San Francisco

San Francisco

By Howard Wilmot

Published by Thomas Cook Publishing
PO Box 227
The Thomas Cook Business Park
Coningsby Road
Peterborough
PE3 8XX

E-mail: books@thomascook.com

ISBN: 1841571 628

Text © 2002 Thomas Cook Publishing
Maps and photographs © 2002 Thomas Cook Publishing

For Thomas Cook Publishing
Managing Director: Kevin Fitzgerald
Publisher: Donald Greig
Commissioning Editor: Deborah Parker
Editor: Sarah Hudson
Proofreader: Ian Kearey

For Pink Paper
General Manager: David Bridle
Publishing Manager: Mike Ross
Editor: Steve Anthony
Additional picture research: Claire Benjamin

Design: Studio 183 and Grassverge
Layout: Studio 183, Peterborough
Cover Design: Studio 183 and Grassverge
Cover Artwork: Steve Clarke, Studio 183

City maps drawn by: Steve Munns
Transport maps: Transport Cartographic Service
Map checker: Colin Follett

Scanning: Dale Carrington, Chronos Publishing; David Bruce Graphics

Printed and bound in Spain by: Artes Gráficas Elkar, Loiu, Spain

Written and researched by Howard Wilmot

Photography: Mark O'Flaherty

The photographers and organisations below are thanked for supplying the following
photographs, to whom the copyright belongs:
San Francisco Convention and Visitors Bureau: pages 14 (Union Square), 18, 72.
Neil Setchfield: pages 6 (statue), 119, 124, 125, 127, 128.
W San Francisco Hotel: pages 92, 116.

Cover photographs: Mark O'Flaherty, Scott Nunn
Main cover photograph: Spectrum Colour Library

Contents

CONTENTS

My Kind of Town...

The first time I went to San Francisco was when I was 11 years old. OK, so I wasn't hitting the Castro big-style with Mum and Dad in tow, but since then I've been back countless times. It's probably the city I know best out of anywhere I've ever been... and I've been around. I've travelled the States from New Orleans to New York, done the Ibiza thing with the Vengaboys (don't ask!), eaten kim-chi in Korea, taught English in Tokyo, been chucked out of bars in Sydney and had an upset stomach in Indonesia.

I don't know if there's just one thing that makes me go back, but the fact that it's the world's premier gay city sure is seductive. And while San Francisco isn't the busiest or even the most happening of places I've ever visited, it does supply enough scenarios to fulfil any gay fantasy, whether that be a Country and Western club, a swishy up-market drinking venue or even a Latino drag bar.

And as much as there's a rock-solid gay and lesbian community to envy and flirt with, try not to get too carried away and ignore what else makes this city so great: its unique laid-back vibe and atmosphere.

San Francisco is a city that seems not to change much over the years, and I think this guide pretty much has it covered. I want to direct you to the best of the action, not every last store selling every last postcard of the Golden Gate Bridge. So go, and have the time of your life, squeezing as much out of this gay Mecca as time will allow. But remember – you really don't have to wear a flower in your hair these days...

Howard Wilmot would like to thank Eric Charge, Lisa Richards, Anna Lawson and Alex Sanz.

Window shopping in the Castro

Out in San Francisco

So just what is it like to be gay in San Francisco? Well, pretty darn good is the short answer.

San Francisco is arguably the gayest city in the world. With a population of almost 800,000 people, it can boast about a quarter of them as gay and lesbian. Think about that figure for a moment.

It means gay people are integral to the workings of this city and yes, you'll see your pink brothers and sisters driving vans, flipping hamburgers, selling real estate or whatever. You can get the impression that were they all to go on strike, stunning San Francisco would come to a standstill.

Not only has the city got a proud history of tolerance, political activism and radicalism – more of that later – but it has always been home to eccentrics and is famous for being the place where people, straight and gay, come to reinvent themselves – or change their lives entirely. It is, after all, the end of the road; the furthest point west before it is east. You can make it happen here, or go back to Hick Town, Idaho.

Throw in the fact that it's a fascinating melting pot of races, colours and creeds, and you can understand why gay men and women have embraced the city as their own – and why San Francisco has embraced them

right back. What all this means is that you can generally wander around hassle- and abuse-free, and get in taxis with straight drivers who'll happily discuss what happened to 'that bar which used to be gay on Polk Street'.

That's not to say, however, that San Francisco is a 100 per cent total gay paradise. Yes, prejudice still exists. It might not always be cool to be out in some blue-collar jobs, for example, and it's not like you see gay couples holding hands, waving rainbow flags and strutting their stuff along Market Street and through the centre of town on a daily basis. You'll have to wait for the annual Pride Parade for that. But on the whole you will be able to make the most of San Francisco's laid-back atmosphere and *laissez-faire* vibe.

So how did the city get to be like this? Some folk will have you believe that San Francisco has always been gay-friendly – even as far back as the 1849 Gold Rush, when men dug each other as well as the glittery stuff. But the roots of gay liberation probably stretch back before the gay movement really got moving in the 1970s.

San Francisco's endemic literary Beat Generation of the 1950s reflected the unease of a post-war generation, but more importantly

Simply divine

it opened the doors a decade later for the hippie explosion – a counter-cultural, politically active movement that aimed to change the world that gave birth to it.

No wonder then that in this free-thinking, free-loving atmos-phere, a burgeoning gay rights movement began to establish itself. And four years before New York's Stonewall Riots in 1969, San Francisco was home to an event which really kick-started the gay movement.

Being gay back in the 1960s was not a barrel of laughs. Gay bars were frequently raided and police harassment on the streets was common.

It was in 1964 that the Council on Religion and the Homosexual was formed, and their first fund-raising event was a New Year's Eve dance at California Hall on Polk Street. On that evening, plain-clothes police descended upon the event, harassing and photographing the 500 revellers who went in, eventually arresting four people. The next day a press conference was called by the Council on Religion and the Homosexual, and the American Civil Liberties Union soon took up the case. This resulted in the acquittal of the four – and

amounted to the community's first taste of real power.

No wonder then that a decade later the city's gay activists were making headway in local politics: the Society for Individual Rights' Jim Foster was the first openly-gay delegate at a Democratic Convention, while legendary campaigner Harvey Milk was on the city's Board of Advisers.

Also on the Board of Supervisors had been anti-gay conservative Daniel White. He was forced to resign because of unstable mental health, and though he'd petitioned to be reinstated, Harvey Milk had persuaded Mayor George Moscone not to open the doors to the man again. As a result, on 28 November 1978, White shot and killed both of them.

In the ensuing court case, White was convicted of manslaughter and sentenced to five years with parole. Cue outrage across the city and the very public storming of City Hall. During his time, Harvey Milk had sponsored one law barring anti-gay discrimination, but more than that, he'd proved that a gay person could succeed in public office.

Segue to the arrival of AIDS at the end of the 1970s. The toll the epidemic has taken on the city and the gay community has been without doubt horrific, but it has lead to a renewed militant AIDS activism, the mobilisation of volunteers and a strong support network for people with HIV/AIDS.

Which brings us back to the here and now.

You'll find San Francisco is a city which celebrates its gay

Rainbow dragon

community. June is Gay, Lesbian, Bisexual and Transgender Pride month, which sees a host of gay events such as the Lesbian and Gay Film Festival. The festival climaxes with the Gay Pride Parade through the heart of the city to the Embarcadero, which is topped with a mammoth party. It's the city's most popular ritual, though there are a series of other events also worth mentioning, such as the Harvey Milk Memorial March in November, and the AIDS Candlelight March in May, as well as more light-hearted events like Folsom Street Fair at the end of September and the Castro Street Fair at the beginning of October. See page 150 for more.

Although the Mission and Castro districts might hint at the ghettoisation of lesbians and gay men respectively, they live there mainly because it's practical and convenient. And in each area the community is possibly more diverse than any other, as it cuts across race, class and creed. Here you're likely to find a wealth of experiences, whether that's an Hispanic bar, a book club meeting, a leather club, a lesbian mums' association or a transgender support group.

If you are visiting from gay meccas like London or New York and hanging out on the scene here, it can feel surprisingly small-town – or even parochial. But you are ignoring what is truly unique about this amazing city – which is being able to get on with your life without your sexuality ever having to be an issue.

Travel by tram

Stepping Out

The beauty of San Francisco is that you don't feel like you have to tick off a list of sightseeing spots to appreciate its beauty. It's a pick'n'mix of a city which throws different communities, flavours and attitudes into the pot. While the recommendations below will help you feel like you have done the city justice, you'll get just as much satisfaction from relaxing into San Francisco's laid-back vibe.

My Top Sights

SFMoMA and Yerba Buena Gardens

SFMoMA. 151 3rd Street, between Minna and Howard Streets. *See map p. 46* 415-357-4000 www.sfmoma.org BART Montgomery Street; Muni Metro F, J, K, L, M, N 11am–5.45pm Mon–Wed and Fri–Sun; 11am–8.45pm Thu; 10am Memorial Day–Labor Day Adults $9; first Tues free

Yerba Buena Center for the Arts. 701 Mission Street at 3rd Street. *See map p. 46* 415-978-2787 BART Montgomery Street; Muni Metro F, J, K, L, M, N 11am–6pm Tues–Sun $7

Yerba Buena Gardens: 3rd and 4th Streets, between Mission and Folsom Streets. *See map p. 46* 415-541-0312 BART Montgomery Street; Muni Metro F, J, K, L, M, N

Metreon: 221 4th Street at Mission Street. *See map p. 46* 415-369-6000 www.metreon.com BART Powell Street; Muni Metro F, J, K, L, M; bus 9, 14, 30, 45; cable car Powell-Mason, Powell-Hyde 10am–10pm daily

These attractions now occupy one of the most interesting blocks in the city, a recent development which has proven a major tourist draw. SFMoMA stands for San Francisco Museum of Modern Art, and the mid-1990s saw it move to its current location. The gallery boasts painting, sculpture, architecture and media arts, and includes works by such heavyweights as Matisse, Pollock, Miró and Klee. Across the street sits Yerba Buena Gardens, a futuristic vision of a park. The nearby Moscone Convention Center looks like something out of the movie *Logan's Run*, and the huge Sony complex, Metreon, has 15 cinemas as well as an IMAX theatre. If this is the future, bring it on.

STEPPING OUT

Great Views

Coit Tower: | **ⓘ** Telegraph Hill. *See map p. 34* | **📷** 415-362-0808 | **🚌** Bus 39 | **🕐** 10am–5pm daily | **💲** $3

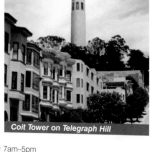
Coit Tower on Telegraph Hill

Twin Peaks: | **ⓘ** Twin Peaks Boulevard, off Portola Drive, between Glenview Drive and Woodside Avenue. *See map p. 70* | **🚌** Bus 36, 37

Transamerica Pyramid: | **ⓘ** 600 Montgomery Street. *See map p. 34* | **📷** 415-983-4100 | **🚌** BART Embarcadero; Muni Metro F, J, K, L, M; bus 1, 9, 30, 41 | **🕐** 7am–5pm

Top Of The Mark: | **ⓘ** Mark Hopkins Hotel, 1 Nob Hill. *See map p. 46* | **📷** 415-392-3434 | **🚌** Cable car Mason-Powell or California | **🕐** 3pm–12.30am Mon–Sat; 4.30pm–12.30am Sun | **💲** $8 Sun–Thu; $10 Fri–Sat

If you thought San Francisco was beautiful from ground level, it excels on high. Little wonder then that the city offers a selection of opportunities to give it the once over from above.

Coit Tower on Telegraph Hill is probably your best bet. It's a 64-metre concrete tower built by City Hall architect Arthur Brown, while Twin Peaks are two mountains beyond the Castro which will give you a view along Market Street on a clear day – though it is a bit of a schlep.

If you're downtown you can always slip inside San Francisco's most controversial building, the Transamerica Pyramid, and check out the city view from the 27th floor. A good vantage point is also to be had from Nob Hill, though the Top Of The Mark bar in the Mark Hopkins Hotel takes it one step further, allowing you the opportunity to enjoy the experience with a cocktail, even if it is in fusty surroundings and at a price!

Union Square

🚌 Bus 2, 3, 4, 30, 38, 45, 76; cable car Powell-Hyde, Powell-Mason. *See map p. 20*

Heart of the city

At the time of writing, Union Square was in the process of getting a facelift. But whatever its cosmetic state, the downtown destination is still the hottest block in the city, filled as it is with hotels, shops and tourists. And there are lots of them. Bordered by Stockton, Powell, Post and Geary, the square and its surrounding streets are home to the States' premier department stores like Macy's, Neiman Marcus and Saks Fifth Avenue, as well as the world's biggest and most exclusive brands like Niketown, Levi Strauss, Tiffany, Gucci, Louis Vuitton and the like. The theatre district is just a stone's throw away, as are the majority of San Francisco's upwardly mobile hotels.

Golden Gate Park and California Academy of Sciences

Golden Gate Park: Between Fulton and Stanyan Streets, Lincoln Way and the Great Highway. *See map p. 78* Muni Metro N; bus 5, 21 Dawn–dusk daily Free

California Academy of Sciences: Golden Gate Park 415-750-7145 Muni Metro N; bus 5, 21 10am–5pm daily Labor Day–Memorial Day; 9am–6pm daily Memorial Day–Labor Day $8

Vital statistics of the famous bridge

Although you can't access the Golden Gate Bridge from the park, the latter is just as impressive as San Francisco's iconic landmark. It's one of the world's greatest urban parks at three miles long and half a mile wide.

Not surprisingly, it encompasses everything you could ever wish for in a city green space, and is home to must-see features like the Japanese Tea Gardens, Strybing Arboretum, the AIDS grove... the list goes on. Come in the summer and you'll see all of San Francisco at play. Note: parking is difficult, so come by public transport.

The park also features the California Academy of Sciences, which in turn promises 'Earth. Ocean. Space. All in one place', thanks to its amalgamation of the Morrison Planetarium, Steinhart Aquarium and the Natural History Museum. You don't have to be a kid to be impressed. See Golden Gate Park, page 73, for more information.

Get Out of Town

Angel Island: Blue and Gold Fleet from Pier 41, Embarcadero 415-705 5555 Bus 32, 42; cable car Powell-Mason Two to three departures daily Ferry: $10.50
Berkeley: BART at Berkeley
Sausalito: Blue & Gold Fleet from Pier 41, Embarcadero 415-705 5555 Bus 32, 42; cable car Powell-Mason Departures every 90 minutes or so Ferry: $6 one-way

As beautiful as San Francisco is, there's a wealth of delights not too far out of town. The best are probably the following.

Angel Island might not be the most obvious (or essential) of sightseeing spots, but it'll give you a refreshing burst of Californian countryside just a 20-minute ferry ride from the city.

Berkeley is much more than a world-famous university town. Yes, the university is definitely worth giving the once-over, but don't ignore its varied bookshops and gourmet restaurants.

Sausalito is a tourist favourite. A former fishing village, it's very picturesque, with delightful bungalows, charming restaurants and some of the most gorgeous views of the city.

Alcatraz Island

ℹ️ Blue and Gold Ferry from Pier 41, Embarcadero. *See map p. 28* 📞 415-705-5555 🚌 Bus 32, 42; cable car Powell-Mason ⏰ From 9.30am daily 💲 $13.25 – book in advance in high season

There's no escape

Alcatraz is perhaps the most famous former jail in the world. Its name, taken from the Spanish for 'pelican', has become notorious since it housed the States' most hardened criminals, including Machine Gun Kelly, Robert 'The Birdman' Stroud and Al Capone, who apparently lost his mind as well as his liberty there.

The island first became a prison back in 1854, but came into its own after the 1906 earthquake, promising unrelentingly hellish and inescapable conditions. It closed its doors in 1963, but became home to a two-year occupation by Native Americans in 1969, a protest still honoured today with an annual Unthanksgiving ceremony in November. Find it all out for yourself in a series of talks, films, exhibitions and a tour around the rock. See Alcatraz, page 30, for further information.

Golden Gate Bridge

Symbol of the city

ℹ️ Access from the Toll Plaza at the Presidio. *See map p. 74* 📞 415-921-5858 🚌 Bus 10, 20, 28 to the bridge 💲 Toll: $3 for vehicles

Think of San Francisco and you think of its ubiquitous symbol, the Golden Gate Bridge. And of all these recommendations, the rusty-coloured icon is the one thing you've pretty much got to see. Beautiful in full-on sunshine or – what's more likely – swathed in fog, you can catch a view of it from various places across the city, so don't feel like you have to get up close.

Linking San Francisco with Marin County, the span was completed in 1937 at a cost of $35 million. The construction claimed 11 lives, is over a mile long and is continuously repainted with 5,000 gallons of International Orange to blend in with its surroundings. But yes, you can walk across it. It takes about an hour and it's freezing – even in the height of summer. See Presidio and Golden Gate Bridge, page 69, for further details.

Civic Center

City Hall:  1 Dr Carlton B Goodlett Place . *See map p. 56* 415-554-4000 Bus 5, 21 8am–8pm Mon–Fri; noon–4pm Sat Free

Civic Center is home to the offices of the city government, as well as many of its arts and performance centres. It's an impressive array of Beaux Arts buildings, which are the setting for festivals and demonstrations. It's well worth a peek if you're passing.

The jewel in its concrete crown is City Hall, which has survived three fires and a major earthquake, and recently underwent a $300 million makeover. It features a jaw-dropping 24-carat gilded dome, and you can wander around for free inside, as it also houses rolling exhibitions.

Cable Car Rides

6am–1am daily $2 one-way

Take a ride

Cable cars are as symbolic of San Francisco as red double-decker buses are in London, or yellow taxis in New York. Riding one is a most enjoyable experience. Originally there were 30 lines, but only three survive. The trio were revived in 1984 for a pretty penny, and comprise the Powell-Mason, Powell-Hyde and the California lines, the last running between Market Street and Van Ness Avenue. The stops are marked by pole-mounted signs. The Powell-Hyde line offers the best views and so is usually packed, with tourists even hanging off the side. It'll take you to Fisherman's Wharf.

The Castro

If San Francisco is the gay capital of the States, The Castro (Muni Metro F, K, L, M; bus 24, 33, 35, 37) is the epicentre of the capital. For gay visitors, its rainbow-flagged streets are a must. At the end of Market Street, the area was originally a Mexican ranch populated by Irish immigrants until its first gay drinkerie, the Twin Peaks Bar, scared everyone off. Though the stores offer niche-targeted merchandise, you can also find gay-run cafés, pharmacies, clothes stores, in fact the lot. If you've ever wondered what the world would look like if it were gay, then this is it. *See also p. 69.*

Home to the largest population of Chinese people outside China

Around Town

What is unique about San Francisco is that although it's a small city, it divides into different communities in a way that cities tend not to in Europe. The following chapter should not only give you a geographical overview of the city but a varied taste of what's on offer. Not all the areas have specific gay relevance, but if you really want to live the life while you're here then head straight for the Castro and the Mission, otherwise pick and choose the areas you think will float your boat.

Downtown

Downtown San Francisco covers seven square miles or so, and it's a varied area, offering a cross-section of what the city has to offer, from the business-like Financial District through swanky Nob Hill to the ratty Tenderloin area. Allow yourself at least a couple of days to cover the area between Embarcadero, Van Ness and Market Street.

Union Square, Chinatown and North Beach

Once the home of pro-Union marches, Union Square and the area around it is now a fantastic shopping destination, providing you with every opportunity to do some damage to your plastic pal in its upmarket shops, department stores, chains and designer emporiums.

Chinatown is home to the largest urban population of Chinese people outside China. The Cantonese first started settling here in the 1840s after escaping famine and opium wars at home, and once they'd put down their roots, even the 1906 earthquake and fire couldn't shake them.

Ultimately, the area doesn't offer much more than a slew of tourist shops (slippers, backscratchers, chirping grasshoppers – you know the deal), average restaurants, herbalists, 'antique' shops and a selection of fresh produce markets. You'll more than likely hit it en route to somewhere else at some point, which is probably the best way to approach it.

North Beach is unmissable, however. Home to the city's oldest Italian community, it welcomed bohemians in the 1950s, the Beatniks and the hippies in the 60s, and is now also populated by the Chinese. It might be a prime tourist spot with a European feel, but it maintains its authenticity.

Union Square, Chinatown and North Beach

You simply have to eat or drink something here, and with its Italian heritage, pizza, pasta and cappuccinos are the order of the day. The restaurants and cafés here are possibly the best and most varied of anywhere in the States.

A DAY OUT

Union Square is a cinch to get to, as most modes of transport will take you there, and more than likely it's also where your hotel is situated. Depending on how hardened a shopaholic you are, perusing Union Square (bordered by Powell, Stockton, Geary and Post Streets) can take anything from a morning to a whole day.

Unless you're here for the sales, don't expect to find too many bargains, as this is the destination for top-end designers like Gucci as well as America's favourite swanky department stores like Macy's, Neiman Marcus and Saks Fifth Avenue – though no Barney's, we're afraid. There are, however, several standard chain outlets around the square like Borders, Levi's Store and Niketown, who have all moved in recent years to take advantage of the prestigious address.

Check out the surrounding streets for more of the same as well as street cafés, news-stands, flower stalls and mini malls, though the most interesting walkways are Maiden Lane to the east of the Square and Claude Lane to the north. Both are chic, pedestrianised affairs and home to less mainstream stores and cafés – you'll even find the city's only Frank Lloyd Wright-designed building at 140 Maiden Lane.

Walk three blocks east to experience the Crocker Galleria if you're really a Versace or Ralph Lauren devotee, but for further shopping opportunities, head south along Powell Street to the multi-tiered San Francisco Shopping Center on Market Street, which is actually more stylish than department store Nordstrom and the mid-range shops it houses. En route you'll discover the Powell Street Cable Car Turnaround where you can pick up two of the three world-famous lines, which will take you to either Fisherman's Wharf or Ghiradelli Square. There are usually lengthy queues, so do as the locals do and walk up a couple of blocks to pick up the tram there.

Shopping at Saks

As soon as you're tired of shopping, walk

north along Grant Avenue and you'll come to the Chinatown Gateway at Bush – you can't miss its traditional ornate structure with good luck symbols. A symbol of Chinatown, you might want to get your photograph taken here.

Grant Avenue is the area's main drag. Once a collection of opium dens, bordellos and gambling joints, it's now a trashy tourist trap offering more tack than you can shake a backscratcher at – but even if you're not going to buy anything, it's an interesting enough distraction for a while. One block north from the Chinatown Gateway, you'll discover Old St Mary's Cathedral, which offers a sense of calm compared to the bustle outside.

Turn right off Grant at Clay Street and you'll discover Portsmouth Plaza on top of an underground car park. Despite its status as the birthplace of the modern city, it's a fairly unprepossessing area, boasting an open space with a playground where locals hang out, though it's also the spot to check out all sorts of Chinese merriment at key times.

If you're a diehard fan of all things Chinese, build into your schedule time for the tiny Kong Chow and Tin How Temples on Stockton Street and Waverly Place on your way here, as well as the Chinese Cultural Center on Kearny Street, opposite Portsmouth Plaza.

From Chinatown walk east to Columbus Avenue, which is as good a place to start exploring North Beach as any. It and the surrounding streets are packed with restaurants, cafés and delis (with tables outside during the warmer months), and whether you're after gourmet or traditional Italian food, it's pretty hard to go wrong here – particularly noteworthy is Caffè Trieste on Vallejo Street (off Columbus), which is the oldest coffee shop in the city and a cool place to stop off.

North Beach is also famous for its Beatnik roots, and whether you're interested in the movement or not, an essential stop-off further up Columbus is the eclectic and renowned bookshop City Lights, which dates from the era.

Further along, the heart of North Beach beats at Washington Square Park. Bordered by yet more restaurants, the grassy square sees the locals sunbathing, hooking up with friends or just putting their feet up. You might want to as well.

Overlooking the park are the church towers of St Peter and St Paul. With a clean white Romanesque-looking façade, the 'Italian Cathedral' was the location for Marilyn Monroe and Joe DiMaggio's wedding photos, no less.

Signs and symbols

Out to Lunch

Near Union Square there is **Cafe De La Presse** (352 Grant Avenue at Bush Street; tel 415-392-3505; *see p. 98*), a sparklingly clean French café which will satisfy you on a coffee and lunch basis, while **Mocca** at 175 Maiden Lane (open 9.30am–4.30pm daily) offers a deli-inspired selection of salads and sandwiches.

In North Beach, your choice of cafés is a varied one, though **Caffè Trieste** (601 Vallejo Street at Grant Avenue; *see p. 98*) is still a real winner for a quick caffeine fix. It's an authentically hip little joint which will also serve you pizza, toasted sandwiches, pastries and antipasti. If you're dying to do *dim sum* in Chinatown, choose carefully – ironically, you're not going to find the best Chinese fare here. Nevertheless, **You's Dim Sum** (675 Broadway: *see p. 100*) is a straightforward but tasty experience.

OUTLINES

BORDERS

🛈 Union Square, corner Powell and Post Streets

📞 415-399-1633

🚇 BART Powell Street; Muni Metro F, J, K, L, M, N; cable car Powell-Mason, Powell-Hyde; Bus 2, 3, 4, 76

🕙 9am–11pm Mon–Wed; 9am–midnight Thu–Sat; 9am–9pm Sun

If you want main-stream tomes, mags etc, here's your place.

CHINATOWN GATEWAY

🛈 Grant Avenue at Bush Street

🚇 Bus 2, 3, 4, 15, 30, 45

Also known as the 'Dragon's Gate', this southern gateway to Chinatown has good luck symbols.

CHINESE CULTURAL CENTER

🛈 750 Kearny Street

📞 415-986-1822

🚇 Bus 1, 15, 30, 45

🕙 10am–4pm Tues–Sun

Open since 1973, the Center aims to preserve, promote and influence the course of Chinese and Chinese-American culture with educational program-mes, exhibitions, events and performances.

CITY LIGHTS

🛈 261 Columbus Avenue between Broadway and Pacific Street

📞 415-362-8193

🚇 Bus 12, 15, 41, 83

🕙 10am–midnight daily

Considered by most San Franciscans the best bookstore in town. Owned by poet Lawrence Ferlinghetti, City Lights comes complete with a high-brow but laid-back atmosphere. Don't miss the basement.

CROCKER GALLERIA

🛈 50 Post Street

📞 415-989-1412

🚇 Bus 2, 4, 5, 30, 38

🕙 10am–6pm Mon–Fri; 10am–5pm Sat

A shopping centre with over 50 outlets catering to the high-end market with designer and boutique stores and restaurants.

GUCCI

🛈 200 Stockton Street

📞 415-392-2808

🚇 Bus 2, 3, 4, 30, 38, 45

🕙 10am–6pm Mon–Sat; noon–6pm Sun

Not the biggest Gucci store ever, but it's substantial enough to cater to all your designer needs.

KONG CHOW TEMPLE

- 855 Stockton Street
- 415-434 2513
- Bus 1, 30, 45
- 10am-4pm daily

Possibly the oldest altar and statuary in North America are housed in this modern temple.

LEVI'S STORE

- 300 Post Street
- 415-501-0100
- BART Powell Station; cable car Powell-Mason, Powell-Hyde; bus 2, 3, 4, 9, 9AX, 38, 76
- 10am-8pm Mon-Sat; 11am-6pm Sun

With the company's home being San Francisco, you'd expect it to impress, and it does with several levels of 501s, twisted cuts and fashion ranges.

MACY'S

- 170 O'Farrell Street
- 415-397-3333
- BART Montgomery Street; cable car Powell-Mason or Powell-Hyde; Muni Metro F, J, K, L, M, N; bus 2, 3, 4, 38, 45
- 10am-8pm Mon-Sat; 11am-7pm Sun

Spanning two city blocks, the men's store features a street café and a great selection of underwear.

NEIMAN MARCUS

- 150 Stockton Street
- 415-362-3900
- BART Montgomery Street; cable car Powell-Mason or Powell-Hyde, Muni Metro F, J, K, L, M, N; bus 2, 3, 4, 38, 45
- 10am-7pm Mon-Wed, Fri & Sat; 10am-8pm Thu; noon-6pm Sun

'Needless mark-up' is the gag, but they can

San Francisco – home of the denim pioneer

get away with it in this flash store. Good menswear department, which also features tasty skincare goodies. Treat yourself to something bad for you in the upstairs Rotunda Café.

Niketown

NIKETOWN

ⓘ 278 Post Street
☎ 415-392-6453
Ⓜ BART Powell Station; cable car Powell-Mason, Powell-Hyde; bus 2, 3, 4, 9, 9AX, 38, 76
⊛ 10am–8pm Mon–Sat; 11am–7pm Sun

What you've come to expect from the kings of global branding: part sportswear emporium, part marketing fest.

OLD ST MARY'S CATHEDRAL

ⓘ 660 California Street
☎ 415-288-3800
Ⓜ Bus 1, 15, 30, 45
⊛ 7am–7pm Mon–Fri; 10am–7pm Sat; 8am–5pm Sun

The first Catholic cathedral in San Francisco, this is a redbrick outfit that has been ravaged by fire twice.

PORTSMOUTH PLAZA

ⓘ Kearny/Clay Street
Ⓜ Bus 1, 15

The historical centre, this is where the Mexican village Yerba Buena stood before being claimed by the Americans in 1846. It is now the social centre of Chinatown.

ST PETER/ST PAUL

ⓘ 666 Filbert Street
☎ 415-421-0809
Ⓜ Bus 15, 30, 39, 45

Known as the Italian Cathedral or Fisherman's Church, it was completed in 1924 and has ornate decoration and a vast, stunning mural of Christ.

SAKS FIFTH AVENUE

ⓘ 220 Post Street
☎ 415-986-4300
Ⓜ Muni Metro F, J, K, L, M, N; cable car Powell-Mason, Powell-Hyde; bus 2, 3, 38, 45
⊛ 10am–7pm Mon–Wed and Sat; 10am–8pm Thu–Fri; noon–6pm Sun

Saks is the *crème de la crème* of department stores. The menswear store is separate and mixes luxury with fashion.

TIN HOW TEMPLE

ⓘ 125 Waverly Place
Ⓜ Bus 1, 15, 30, 45
⊛ 10am–5pm daily

This tiny temple has been operating since 1852. It's at the top of three steep flights of stairs. Breathe in the atmosphere once you make it.

WASHINGTON SQUARE

ⓘ Stockton Street and Union Street
Ⓜ Bus 15, 30, 39, 45

A statue of Benjamin Franklin presides over this small but cute park and local neighbourhood hangout.

PIER 39

SEA LIONS /
VIOLATION OF
THE MARINE
MAMMAL
PROTECTION ACT

Pier 39 – as laid-back as the rest of the city

Fisherman's Wharf and Alcatraz

Visit Fisherman's Wharf if you really, really must, but it's essentially a tatty-looking tourist trap. Though you can still see fishermen bringing in today's fresh catches in the early morning on Fish Alley, just off Jefferson Street, tourists move in throughout the day to board ferries, eat at overpriced restaurants and shop at tacky joints on Pier 39 and the surrounding area. There's a selection of other 'tourist-only' features too including the Wax Museum at Fisherman's Wharf, a Rainforest Café, Underwater World and Namcoland.

It's near here, however, that you board ferries for Alcatraz. It might have shut up shop as a prison back in 1963, but its legend lives on with over a million visitors a year. So yes, you can expect crowds and you will have to book in advance – the inconvenience of which will depend on the season. It's also pretty chilly out there, even in the summer, so come prepared.

A DAY OUT

If you're doing the tourist thing, you might want to take one of the cable cars to Fisherman's Wharf. Both Powell-Mason and Powell-Hyde, which run along said streets, give you the opportunity.

Shopping is the main deal along Fisherman's Wharf, but whether you'll find anything of value or quality is questionable. Hit the wharf and you hit tourist central, but on a sunny day there are worse ways to kill time.

Local delight: sourdough bread and clam chowder

Most of the action takes place at Pier 39 (for which the Powell-Mason line is your best bet). Once a working pier, it's now a shabby-looking shopping mall offering shops with names like Shell Cellar, A Bug And Beyond, and Midsummer Night's Lingerie. Tacky isn't the word. Off Pier 39 you'll see the famed colony of sea lions basking on the docks.

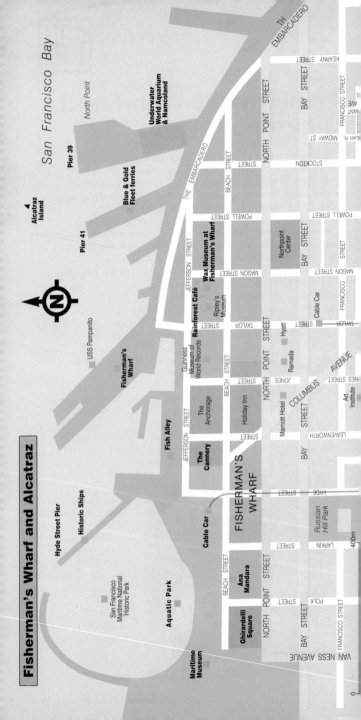

Fisherman's Wharf and Alcatraz

San Francisco Bay

North Point

Alcatraz Island

Pier 39

Pier 41

Underwater World Aquarium & Namcoland

Blue & Gold Fleet ferries

THE EMBARCADERO

USS Pampanito

Fisherman's Wharf

Fish Alley

Hyde Street Pier

Historic Ships

San Francisco Maritime National Historic Park

Aquatic Park

Maritime Museum

Wax Museum at Fisherman's Wharf

Rainforest Café

Ripley's Museum

Guinness Museum of World Records

The Cannery

The Anchorage

Northpoint Center

Holiday Inn

Marriott Hotel

Hyatt

Ramada

Art Institute

Cable Car

Ghirardelli Square

Ana Mandara

Russian Hill Park

FISHERMAN'S WHARF

JEFFERSON STREET

BEACH STREET

NORTH POINT STREET

BAY STREET

JONES STREET

LEAVENWORTH STREET

COLUMBUS AVENUE

HYDE STREET

LARKIN STREET

POLK STREET

VAN NESS AVENUE

FRANCISCO STREET

TAYLOR STREET

MASON STREET

POWELL STREET

STOCKTON

MIDWAY ST

KEARNY STREET

FRANCISCO STREET

0   400m

FISHERMAN'S WHARF AND ALCATRAZ

Wander east along Jefferson Street and among the shops, restaurants and erm... amusements like the Wax Museum (which offers a couple of examples in a revolving glass showcase), you'll find fresh seafood stalls which also sell the area's famed sourdough bread, sometimes hollowed out and filled with anaemic-looking clam chowder. Sample it if you dare.

The Cannery and Ghiradelli Square are a couple of nearby shopping centres which you'll hit as you work your way west away from Pier 39, however. They offer vaguely more palatable products. But don't hold your breath.

Your best bet in the area is the green space known as Aquatic Park, almost opposite Ghiradelli. It's well worth a wander for its fabulous views across the sailing-boat-studded bay to Golden Gate Bridge and Alcatraz. The Maritime Museum stands at the corner, acting as a showcase for

En route to Alcatraz

replica boats, bells and mastheads, while the nearby Hyde Street Pier features an extensive selection of Historic Ships dating back to the 19th century.

If you want to avoid all the above nonsense, book your trip for Alcatraz over the phone or internet in advance, so you don't have to kill time in the area. If you're at Aquatic Park however, a good idea is to wander back to Pier 41, where you can pick up the ferry for the 20-minute (or so) ride.

The prison will no doubt fill the best part of half a day, though there are also night tours if you want to give your visit a spooky spin, and combo deals where you can take in another sightseeing hotspot like Sausalito. The Blue and Gold Fleet ferries, departing from Pier 41 on Fisherman's Wharf up to 16 times a day, will drop you off on Alcatraz.

On your arrival at the quay, a 'prison guard' will fill you in on all the dos and don'ts, but before you head up the hill to explore, there is a short movie and museum to give you its history. There are also daily events where former prison guards and ex-prisoners will give you a more subjective view.

On entering the massive jail, you'll be given a complimentary audio tour guide, which will not only guide you around the site but also give you all the interesting background stories – it's worth it, too. As you wander around the dank and empty buildings, you'll be able to check out solitary confinement, the dining room, gun gallery and the cheerless cells in their original state. Grim, but endlessly fascinating.

Out to Lunch

There are loads of opportunities to sup overpriced but totally average food along the Waterfront. And as tempting as it might be to try the traditional West Coast chowder (which is different to the East Coast variety), try to resist. Locals wouldn't be seen dead eating out here – except at the upmarket and totally delicious **Ana Mandara** (891 Beach Street; *see p. 93*). A vast soundstage of a restaurant, Ana Mandara nevertheless provides a top-quality (and correspondingly pricey) experience of modern Vietnamese in what is a culinary wasteland.

Fast food on the Waterfront

Over on Alcatraz, it's no better. As it's a national park, there's no food or drink for sale on the island, and you're not allowed to bring any in case it makes the resident seagulls ill, so it's worth making sure you're fed and watered before getting on that ferry, although if you're desperate the boat itself offers cold drinks, snacks and hot dogs.

OUTLINES

ALCATRAZ ISLAND

 📞 415-705-5555
 🚢 Ferry from Pier 41
 ⏱ 9.30am–6.30pm
daily in summer; 9.30am–
4.30pm daily in autumn, winter and spring. Evening tours also available

One of San Francisco's don't-miss attractions. Go ahead and believe all the hype, and make sure you don't miss out on the audio tour for those grim stories (see page 29).

AQUATIC PARK

 ℹ Between Hyde Street and Van Ness Avenue
 🚋 Cable car Powell-Hyde, Powell-Mason; bus 19, 30, 32, 42

In tourist trap central, this green space is very welcome. Stretch your legs or take time out here.

Where's the Birdman?

Aquatic Park

THE CANNERY

ℹ️ 2801 Leavenworth Street

📞 415-771-3112
www.thecannery.com

🚋 Cable car Powell-Hyde, Powell-Mason; bus 19, 30, 32, 42

🕐 10am–6pm Mon–Sat; 11am–6pm Sun

Built in 1909, this mall is a renovated Del Monte fruit-canning factory with exposed brickwork. Now it is full of shops offering you things you never knew you needed over various levels, some of them open-plan.

GHIRADELLI SQUARE

ℹ️ 900 North Point Street, at Beach, Larkin and Polk Streets

📞 415-775-5500

🚋 Cable car Powell-Hyde, Powell-Mason; bus 19, 30, 32, 42

🕐 10am–9pm Mon–Sat; 10am–6pm Sun

Another renovation, this time a one-time (Ghiradelli) chocolate factory and woollen mill gets the uninspiring mall treatment with US brand stores as well as a cutesy chocolate shop.

MARITIME MUSEUM

ℹ️ Foot of Polk Street at Beach Street

📞 415-561-6662

🚋 Cable car Powell-Hyde, Powell-Mason; bus 19, 30, 32, 42

🕐 10am–5pm daily

🎟️ Free

A sexy, nautical-looking building houses models, masts, nautical instruments, photographs and paintings, which map out San Francisco's maritime history over two floors. Definitely worth a visit.

PIER 39

ℹ️ Jefferson Street

🚋 Cable car Powell-Mason; bus 19, 30, 32, 42

Flying the flag

In 1978 when it was refurbished, it seemed like a cutesy fishing village, but now it's an unashamed – and frankly shabby – tourist trap with themed stores.

THE WAX MUSEUM AT FISHERMAN'S WHARF

ℹ️ 145 Jefferson Street, between Mason and Taylor Streets

📞 800-202-0400

🚋 Cable car Powell-Mason; bus 19, 30, 32, 42

🕐 9am–11pm Sun–Thu; 9am–midnight Fri–Sat

Yes, there are historical, fictional and ghoulish figurines, but Madame Tussauds this ain't, just another example of the area's tourist feeding frenzy.

Ghiradelli Square

The Transamerica Pyramid reaches for the sky

Telegraph Hill, the Embarcadero and Financial District

Telegraph Hill is essentially a pricey residential area, one that derives its name from the site of the West Coast's first telegraph. Dependably hilly, it affords great views of the city, the finest being from Coit Tower.

The nearby and lengthy Embarcadero stretches along the waterfront from Fisherman's Wharf in the north to South Beach in the south. Before the arrival of the Bay and Golden Gate Bridges, it used to be where commuters from Marin and East Bay would access the city. It's been overhauled in the not-too-distant past, and now offers prime views across the bay. At best, it's a graceful boulevard, at worst it's a glorified freeway. But whatever your opinion, you'll probably want to saunter/cycle/rollerblade along here for at least 20 minutes or so.

The Financial District is just that: the city's business centre. Full of office workers, it therefore doesn't rate too highly with tourists – except perhaps in the evenings, when top-end restaurants and bars cater for more than just business people. The area smells of money, but also showcases the super-modern and historic buildings San Francisco has on offer.

A DAY OUT

Telegraph Hill is essentially all about the views of the bay and the city, so if you've had your fill elsewhere bypass it and head straight for the Financial District.

To get to Telegraph Hill, you need to pick up the 39 bus from Fisherman's Wharf (*see p. 27*), though you can walk it thanks to either the Filbert or Greenwich Steps off Montgomery Street – the wooden Filbert

Sculpture at the Embarcadero

Telegraph Hill, Embarcadero & Financial District

0 ___ 500
0 ___ 500 yds

Bay Cruises

THE EMBARCADERO

FRANCISCO ST
CHESTNUT STREET

Fog City Diner

LOMBARD STREET

MONTGOMERY STREET

SANSOME STREET

TELEGRAPH HILL

Coit Tower

GREENWICH ST

TELEGRAPH HILL BOULEVARD

NAPIER LA

FILBERT STREET

ALTA ST

Levi's Plaza

UNION STREET

CALHOUN TERR

BATTERY STREET

GREEN STREET

SANSOME STREET

NE Waterfront Historical District

VALLEJO STREET

MONTGOMERY STREET

FRONT STREET

San Francisco Bay

N

Pier 7

B R O A D W A Y

Square One

PACIFIC AVENUE

STREET

DAVIS O

Walton Playground

Cypress Club

Jackson Square Historical District

COLUMBUS AVE

Chinese Culture Center

JACKSON STREET

US Custom House

Transamerica Pyramid

WASHINGTON STREET

MERCHANT ST

Pacific Heritage Museum

Golden Gateway Center

CLAY STREET

THE EMBARCADERO

Justin Herman Plaza

World Trade Center

☐ **Ferry Building**

Chinese Historical Society Museum

Embarcadero Center

SACRAMENTO STREET

BATTERY

SACRAMENTO STREET

DRUMM STREET

Wells Fargo Museum

Aqua

DAVIS STREET

Cable Car

CALIFORNIA STREET

SANSOME

FRONT STREET

MARKET STREET

Bank of America

Mandarin Oriental Hotel

PINE STREET

Merchant's Exchange

M EMBARCADERO

Federal Reserve Bank

Jewish Museum

ST

BELDEN

BUSH STREET

MONTGOMERY

Pacific Coast Stock Exchange

FINANCIAL DISTRICT

MISSION STREET

STEUART STREET

THE EMBARCADERO

Rincon Center

SUTTER STREET

FREMONT STREET

MAIN STREET

SPEAR STREET

MARKET STREET

ECKER ST

STEVENSON ST

ANTHONY ST

JESSIE ST

GG University

FIRST STREET

Transbay Terminal

BEALE STREET

SECOND STREET

MONTGOMERY STREET

M

Sheraton Palace Hotel

MISSION STREET

MINNA STREET

NATOMA STREET

HOWARD STREET

FOLSOM STREET

HARRIS

ANNIE ST

ALDRICH ALLEY

Steps are more picturesque, taking you there via a series of cutesy cottages and gardens.

The hill is home to pretty pastel-coloured clapboard houses. Coit Tower, which looks like the top of a firehose, stands in a green space and will give you an even better panorama. While the lobby is free, it'll cost you $3 to ride the lift to the top, but it's well worth it. Impressively floodlit at night, you can check it out from most parts of the city.

From Coit Tower, wander east back down Telegraph Hill and you can check out the last of the city's wooden plank buildings in the tranquil Napier Lane. Keep on going and you'll hit the Embarcadero, where traffic and streetcars give free wheel, but you can wander past a series of still-in-service piers and warehouses with views across the bay.

Head south and after a bit of a schlep – take one of the many street-cars if you can't be bothered – you arrive at the Ferry Building, where you can pick up ferries across the bay, though the ones from Fisherman's Wharf will take you to the top tourist destinations. At the time of writing the building was in a state of renovation, but was looking to become much more than a rush-hour hub in the future.

The long sweep of Telegraph Hill

Opposite the Ferry Building sits Justin Herman Plaza. Its mix of green spaces and concrete walkways mean it's a lunchtime hangout for nearby office workers, though you'll find skateboarders and cyclists also doing their thing here. It's a good starting point from where to acquaint yourself with the Financial District, the area which gives the city its skyline but which is also peppered with a few historical buildings. All the major banks, brokers and law offices are situated here.

Head west along Sacramento Street and you'll find the Embarcadero Center. Housing generic US brand stores, its buildings are a bit dark and uninspiring, but were being promised a makeover at the time of writing.

At 260m high, the nearby Transamerica Pyramid on Montgomery Street is the tallest building in San Francisco and instantly recognisable because of its unusual but fantastic elongated pyramid design. There is a free observation room on the 27th floor, which is open during business hours and is yet to be totally overrun with tourists. On the fringe of the area, the Jackson Square Historical District features a varied but interesting collection of antiques and furniture stores and bookshops.

☕ Out to Lunch

For something snacky or cheap, wander into nearby North Beach. While the Financial District is the best bet for eating out in this area, it does cater to suits and richer tourists who are housed in the nearby Mandarin Oriental Hotel, the Hyatt Regency and the like.

If you're happy to splash out, there are a couple of opportunities: the **Cypress Club** (500 Jackson Street at Montgomery Street; *see p. 100*) continues to work its magic with a wacky but stylish interior and a tasty modern fusion menu.

But if you're a fish aficionado, check out **Aqua** (252 California Street, between Battery and Front Streets; tel 415-956-9662; BART Embarcadero; Metro Muni F, J, K, L, M, N; cable car California; bus 1, 15, 31, 38AX, 42, 80X; open 11.30am–2.30pm Mon–Fri, 5.30–10.30pm Mon–Thu and Sun, 5.30–11pm Sat–Sun). It might not offer bay views, but its inspirational use of local ingredients and attention to detail are pretty special.

The Embarcadero Center

See the Pyramid

OUTLINES

COIT TOWER

🛈 1 Telegraph Hill Boulevard

📞 415-362-0808

🚌 Bus 39

🕑 10am–7.30pm daily in summer; 10am–6pm daily in autumn, winter and spring

Built in 1934 by City Hall architect Arthur Brown, Coit Tower was named after Lilly Hitchcock Coit who apparently had a thing for firemen, hence its shape. The lobby features Mexican painter Diego Rivera's WPA murals (government-commissioned, Depression-era art). There's top San Francisco viewing action from here.

JUSTIN HERMAN PLAZA

🛈 The Embarcadero

🚇 BART California Street; Muni Metro J, K, L, M, N; bus 1, 41

Downtown green space beloved by office workers with takeouts, it's got walkways and the avant-garde *jolie-laide* Vaillancourt Fountain.

NAPIER LANE

🛈 off Montgomery Street

🚌 Bus 39

The last example of the city's trademark wooden plank cottages, dating from the 19th century.

TRANSAMERICA PYRAMID

🛈 600 Montgomery Street

📞 415-983-4100

🚇 BART Embarcadero; Muni Metro F, J, K, L, M; bus 1, 9, 30, 41

🕑 7am–5pm daily

🎟 Free observation deck

Instantly recognisable and offering great views over the city, it's a huge showy spire which caused outrage when it was unveiled in 1972.

The 'nabobs' neighbourhood

Russian Hill, Nob Hill and the Tenderloin

If you feel like you've already done the city's 'greatest hits', both Russian Hill and Nob Hill are home to a couple of hotspots and make for enjoyable strolls.

Russian Hill is named after a group of Russian sailors thought to be buried here. While it's a residential area, your essential stop-off is Lombard Street, the world-famous 'crookedest street on earth'. A couple of blocks west is Polk Street, which is on the up fast, but not really worth going out of your way for just yet.

Nob Hill is one of the ritziest areas in San Francisco. It got its name from rich 'nabobs', who built swish mansions in the area. It is now also home to the city's most upmarket hotels as well as Grace Cathedral, modelled on the great European churches. The hill also affords great views across the city.

Bizarrely, just 15 minutes or so south, Tenderloin is one of the crummiest districts in San Francisco and therefore not really worth spending any time in – though it's also home to some of the city's theatres. It's thought to have got its name from the legs on show here, as this has long been home to the city's hookers, but now comes with hustlers and homeless too.

A DAY OUT

Starting in the north in the swanky end of Russian Hill, Lombard Street is a tourist classic. You'll find its classy curves edged with well-manicured gardens between Hyde and Leavenworth Streets, so don't be too surprised if you have to join a queue to drive down its nine hairpin bends. If you're in a car, get there early or late to avoid the jam. Easier on foot – the Powell-Hyde cable car will drop you off – if not as much fun.

One block north is the San Francisco Art Institute, a prestigious art school, notable for its Spanish colonial-style building and Diego Rivera's *Making of a Mural* erm... mural.

If you're hell-bent on doing some shopping at every turn, head four blocks west to Polk Street, which might just provide you with that unusual piece you've been looking for. A handsome street lined with stores – though thankfully the big-name brands are yet to take a hold here – it features a bunch of eclectic antiques stores, interesting interiors shops and increasingly upmarket eateries, as well as fulfilling the usual neighbourhood needs. Andrew Rothstein's delicious deli, Swallowtail's beautiful antiques and Acorn Books' selection of antiquarian books will give you a taste of the street at its best. However, the further south you

Russian Hill, Nob Hill and the Tenderloin

Ghirardelli Square

NORTH POINT STREET
Marriott Hotel
Ramada
Hyatt
Northpoint Center

VANDEWATER ST

FRANCISCO STREET
Russian Hill Park
San Francisco Art Institute
HOUSTON ST
FRANCISCO STREET
WATER STREET

CHESTNUT STREET
CHESTNUT STREET

RUSSIAN HILL
Lombard Street
POWELL

LOMBARD STREET
LOMBARD STREET
LOMBARD STREET
North Beach Playgroun

FRANKLIN STREET
VAN NESS AVENUE
POLK STREET

GREENWICH STREET
GREENWICH STREET
JANIS
Michelangelo Playground
GREENWICH STREET
PARAISO ST

FILBERT STREET
FILBERT STREET
FILBERT STREET
Washingt Squa

UNION STREET
UNION STREET
UNION STREET

MACONDRAY LANE
TAYLOR STREET
North Beac Museu

GREEN STREET
EASTMAN ST
GREEN STREET
GREEN STREET

Andrew Rothstein and Swallowtail
VALLEJO STREET
VALLEJO STREET
VALLEJO STREET

BROADWAY
WALDO ALLEY
GLOVER ST
B R O A D W A Y
LEVY TUNNEL

Wills Playground
101
PACIFIC AVE
PACIFIC AVENUE
PACIFIC AVENUE
JOHN ST

JACKSON STREET
JACKSON STREET
JACKSON STREET

TURK STREET
Cable Car Museum
Ch Ho

WASHINGTON STREET
WASHINGTON STREET

CLAY STREET
CLAY STREET
CLAY

NOB HILL
PLEASANT ST
TAYLOR STREET
LA

SACRAMENTO STREET
SACRAMENTO STREET

Grace Cathedral
Huntington Square
CUSH
MAN ST
SPROLE LA
Fairmont Hotel

Cable Car
CALIFORNIA STREET
CALIFORNIA STREET
Stou Renais

Acorn Books
Huntington Hotel
Star Court

PINE STREET
PINE STREET
Mark Hopkin Hotel Top Of The Mark

AUSTIN STREET
St Francis Memorial Hospital

BUSH STREET
BUSH STREET

FERN STREET
American Rag
SUTTER STREET
Café Bean
SUTTER STREET

Hospital

POST STREET
POST STREET

GEARY STREET
GEARY STREET

Curran Theater
Geary Theater
Ma

O'FARRELL STREET
Dottie's True Blue Cafe
O'FARRELL STREET

OLIVE STREET
ELLIS STREET
ELLIS STREET
ELLIS

WILLOW STREET
Visitor Information
Ca
Ca

EDDY STREET
EDDY STREET
POWELL STREET
M

TURK STREET
TENDERLOIN

0   300m
0   300 yds

MARKET ST
FIFTH ST
STEVENSON ST

head towards the Tenderloin, the rattier it becomes, so give up as soon as you feel you've gone far enough.

If you're a fan of Armistead Maupin's *Tales of the City* series of books, you might want to do a detour and check out Macondray Lane, which is widely believed to be Barbary Lane in the books.

Nob Hill is a schlep further south, so take a cab or jump on the Powell-Mason cable car a couple of blocks. Grace Cathedral at the top is an architectural delight, overlooking the pretty green Huntington Square. The cathedral is beautifully maintained, with stunning stained glass.

Nob Hill smells of money, and around the square you'll find elegant buildings and the city's ritziest old-school hotels like the Huntington, Fairmont and Stouffer Renaissance Stanford Court – though the most famous and widely credited with the best views of the city is the Mark Hopkins. You can witness the panorama from the penthouse bar, Top Of The Mark, which opened in 1939. But with a generic chintzy hotel feel and middle-aged crowd, it's not the sexiest bar (plus you'll have to pay!).

Continue south and you hit the Tenderloin, dirty, edgy and potentially dangerous, so be careful. However, if you keep to the theatre district, based around Geary Street towards Union Square, you should be OK. The city has long had a strong theatre tradition, and its most famous are the Curran Theater and the Geary Theater.

Out to Lunch

OK, so it's ultimately a teeny-tiny breakfast venue, but **Dottie's True Blue Cafe** (522 Jones Street; *see p. 96)* is a local favourite – always a good sign. Offering very fine French toast, pancakes and other goodies, the charming staff will also serve you up yummy lunchtime fare as the day progresses.

Lunch with the locals

Alternatively, there's the straightforward **Cafe Bean** (754 Post Street; *see p. 101)*, which, in a city over-populated by Starbucks, is a superior, if no-frills, little café which will fulfil your caffeine needs or offer up snacky goodies like sandwiches and fruit salads. If it's a nice day, you'll even be able to sit outside. .

OUTLINES

ACORN BOOKS

ℹ 1436 Polk Street at California Street

✆ 415-563-1736

Ⓜ Cable car California; bus 19

🕐 10.30am–8pm Mon–Sat; noon–7pm Sun

Antiquarian and secondhand bookstore which has a library feel.

AMERICAN RAG

ℹ 1305 Van Ness Avenue

✆ 415-474-5214

Ⓜ Bus 47, 49, 76

🕐 10am–9pm Mon–Sat; noon–7pm Sun

G–Star, Diesel, Paul and Joe and the like rub shoulders with well-maintained secondhand fare in this classy clothes emporium (in a dodgy area).

ANDREW ROTHSTEIN

ℹ 2238 Polk Street, between Vallejo and Green Streets

✆ 415-447-4094

Ⓜ Bus 19, 30X, 42, 76

🕐 11am–9pm Mon–Fri; 11am–8pm Sat–Sun

Clean, white and totally delicious delicatessen on Polk Street.

CURRAN THEATRE

ℹ 445 Geary Street, between Mason and Taylor

✆ 415-551-2000

Ⓜ BART Powell Street; Muni Metro F, J, K, L, M, N; bus 27, 38

Mainstream theatre productions two blocks away from Union Square.

FAIRMONT, HUNTINGTON AND STOUFFER RENAISSANCE STANFORD COURT HOTELS

Fairmont ℹ 950 Mason Street at Sacramento Street

✆ 415-772-5000

Lombard Street – the crookedest street in the world

Huntington 🛈 1075 California Street at Taylor Street 🚗 415-474-5400

Stouffer Renaissance Stanford Court 🛈 905 California Street at Powell Street 🚗 415-989-3500

The most exclusive and expensive accommodation in town.

GEARY THEATRE

🛈 415 Geary Street, between Mason and Taylor Streets

🚗 415-834-3200

🚌 Bus 2, 3, 4, 27, 38

Home to ACT (American Conservatory Theatre), this restored theatre showcases everything from Mamet to Shakespeare.

GRACE CATHEDRAL

🛈 1100 California Street, between Taylor, Jones and Sacramento Streets

🚗 415-749-6300

🚃 Cable car California; bus 1, 27

One of the city's most stunning churches, the Episcopalian church has a façade modelled on Notre Dame in Paris and an entrance based on the Doors of Paradise in the Baptistry in Florence. Don't miss the Keith Haring altarpiece, *The Life of Christ*, dedicated in 1995 by the AIDS Memorial Chapel Project.

LOMBARD STREET

🛈 Between Leavenworth and Hyde Streets

Nine hairpin bends, 27 per cent gradient, 5mph speed limit, the crookedest street in the world is simply a must either on foot or by car.

MARK HOPKINS HOTEL

🛈 1 Nob Hill, at California and Mason Streets

🚗 415-392-3434

🚃 Cable car California; bus 1, 27

The fourth of the big budget hotels on Nob Hill, but with the addition of a fab view from the Top Of The Mark cocktail bar.

SAN FRANCISCO ART INSTITUTE

🛈 800 Chestnut Street

🚗 415-771-7020

🚌 Bus 30

☀ 9am–5pm daily

Less a museum, more one of the city's most desirable art schools. Fantastic Diego Rivera mural though.

SWALLOWTAIL

🛈 2217 Polk Street

🚗 415-567-1555

🚌 Bus 19, 30X, 42, 76

☀ 11am–9pm Mon–Fri; 11am–8pm Sat–Sun

A perfect example of San Francisco's taste for antiques big and small, simple and edgy.

Tales of the City

If you're going to read one book about San Francisco, make it *Tales of the City* by gay author and activist Armistead Maupin. Originally a groundbreaking serialised newspaper column in 1976, the book and its sequels are about a bunch of characters, kooky and otherwise, and their interweaving exploits in the city.

Much of the action takes place at 28 Barbary Lane, home to Mouse and Mrs Madrigal. OK, there's no such place, but its location is widely believed to be Macondray Lane. To check it out, head south on Taylor Street until you hit Green Street, and keep your eye out for the signs.

Sci-fi style showtime at the Metreon

www.outaround.com

SOMA

SOMA is the name for the area South of Market. You'll probably want to spend at least half a day here to do it justice.

It's an area on the up, initially signalled by the arrival of a slew of interesting and hi-tech architecture in the shape of SFMoMA (San Francisco Museum of Modern Art) and the Yerba Buena Gardens complex, which occupy what used to be a rundown area of industrial buildings and warehouses. It also used to go under the less-appealing moniker 'South-of-the-Slot'.

The original industrial look continues the further towards South Beach you head. But even here, you'll witness how the area is being turned into a shiny new batch of warehouse conversions and property developments.

South Beach is home to the original dot.com revolution, which kicked off in its lofts and garrets during the 1990s. With just a sprinkling of life support on Brannan Street, it's hardly worth giving much, if any time to. Yet.

A DAY OUT

Pick up the BART, Muni Metro or buses 9, 15, 30, 45 to SFMoMA, the red-brick modern triumph with a cylindrical skylight. The gallery embodies 'the perfect balance, where architecture and art enrich each other', and is as amazing on the inside as it is on the outside, with 50,000 square feet of galleries on four floors, not to mention interactive features, a wonderful shop and a quality café. Be sure that if it's modern, SFMoMA has it covered.

The Yerba Buena Gardens complex is literally across the road and is surrounded by state-of-the-art buildings, all built in the last decade or so. Put your feet up or have a wander in the multi-tiered Esplanade Gardens with its green spaces, walkways, fountains, water features, restaurants and the obligatory Starbucks.

At the other side of the Esplanade Gardens, you'll find Sony's Metreon, which fills a whole block on 4th Street. Essentially, the steel and glass-fronted futuristic building is an entertainment complex-cum-shopping mall – check out Sony Style if only to remind yourself how cheap technology has become nowadays. And yes, it really does offer competitive prices.

Head south down 4th Street to discover the enormous, *Blade Runner*-esque Moscone Convention Center. It's the futuristic building with a series of flags outside. You're only likely to wander around its exhibition halls if you're here on business, though it's worth giving it the once-over just to check out the forward-thinking architecture. Nearby is the Moscone Ballroom, also part of the convention centre's facilities.

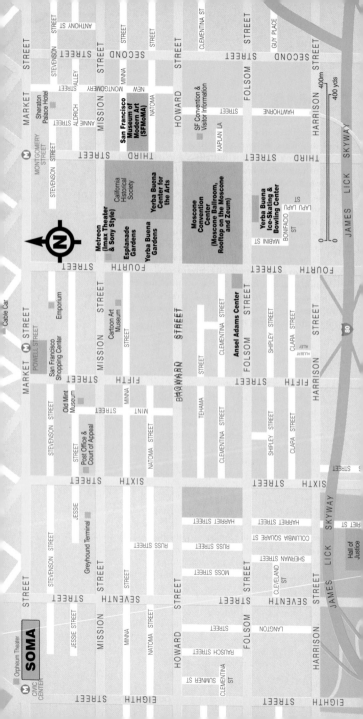

Inhabiting the Rooftop on the Moscone Center is a square block dedicated to youth, with an ice-skating centre, 12-lane bowling alley, carousel and arts and technology museum, Zeum, for kids aged 8–18.

Still have time on your hands? Then here's where you'll also discover the Ansel Adams Center for Photography, dedicated to the work of the prolific photographer plus rolling photographic exhibitions.

Out to Lunch

Café and culture

If you've been perusing the art in SFMoMA, you might as well check out **Caffé Museo**, their top-notch café (151 3rd Street, between Mission and Howard Streets; open 10am–6pm Mon–Tues and Fri–Sun; 10am–9pm Thu; closed Wed and some public holidays). As swish and sexy as you'd expect a state-of-the-art gallery café to be, it also offers a range of interesting and tasty sandwiches, salads and soups, with a queue-busting way of diffusing the lunchtime rush. Outside it's cool and shady, so make the most of it if you come in summer.

OUTLINES

ANSEL ADAMS CENTER

📍 250 Fourth Street, between Folsom and Howard Streets

🌐 415-495-7000
www.friendsofphotograph y.org/

🚌 Bus 9X, 30, 45, 76

🕐 11am–5pm daily; 11am–8pm first Thu of each month 💲 $5

Dig landscape photography? Then pay homage to the master in this stylish gallery. Exhibitions highlight the work of contemporary photographers.

METREON

📍 221 4th Street at Mission Street

🌐 415-369-6000
www.metreon.com

🚇 BART Powell Street; Muni Metro F, J, K, L, M; cable car Powell-Mason, Powell-Hyde; bus 9, 14, 30, 45

🕐 10am–10pm daily

Sony-branded shopping mall-cum-breathtaking entertainment centre overlooking Yerba Buena Gardens. Home to an IMAX

AROUND TOWN

theatre (with a 80ft by 100ft screen), 15 not-to-be-outdone cinemas, plus restaurants and shops like the Discovery Channel store and Sony Style (naturally).

MOSCONE CENTER

ⓘ 747 Howard Street, between 3rd and 4th Streets

☎ 415-974-4000

🚌 Bus 9X, 12, 30, 45, 81X

Keith Haring sculpture opposite SFMoMA

Whopping convention centre named after former Mayor George Moscone. Much of the action takes place underground and over 1.2 million square feet.

SFMOMA

ⓘ 151 3rd Street,

between Minna and Howard Streets

☎ 415-357-4000

www.sfmoma.org

🚇 BART Montgomery Street; Muni Metro F, J, K, L, M, N; bus 9, 15, 30, 45

🕐 11am–5.45pm Mon–Wed and Fri–Sun; 11am–8.45pm Thu; from 10am Memorial Day–Labor Day

🎟 Adults $9; first Tues of each month is free

This impressive Mario Botta-designed modern gallery covers four floors: the second offers the biggest names in modern art – don't miss Jeff Koons' lifesize Michael Jackson figurine – the third photographic works, the fourth hands-on media arts, and the fifth special exhibitions.

YERBA BUENA CENTER FOR THE ARTS

ⓘ 701 Mission Street at 3rd Street

☎ 415-978-2787

🚇 BART Montgomery Street; Muni Metro F, J, K, L, M, N

🕐 11am–6pm Tues–Sun

🎟 $7

Yerba Buena gardens

A smaller but funkier and edgier younger sister to SFMoMA. Fumihiko Maki designed the 755-seat theatre and four galleries, which host constantly changing exhibitions, ranging from pop culture crowd pleasers to more highbrow stuff.

YERBA BUENA GARDENS COMPLEX

ℹ️ 3rd and 4th Streets, between Mission and Folsom Streets

📞 415-541-0312

🚇 BART Montgomery Street; Muni Metro F, J, K, L, M, N

Futuristic park space surrounded by the city's most forward-thinking buildings.

YERBA BUENA ICE-SKATING AND BOWLING CENTER

ℹ️ 750 Folsom Street, between 3rd and 4th Streets

📞 415-777-3727

🚌 Bus 30, 45, 76

🕐 1pm–5pm Mon–Fri; 7.30pm–10.30pm Fri–Sat

💲 $6

Expansive leisure space mainly for the youth market. Plenty of fun to be had.

ZEUM

ℹ️ 221 4th Street at Howard Street

📞 415-777-2800

🚌 Bus 30, 45, 76

🕐 Noon–6pm Wed–Fri; 11am–5pm Sat–Sun

💲 $7

Swish glass-fronted arts and technology museum within the Moscone Center with cutting edge multi-media facilities. Again, something mainly for the kids.

Yerba Buena Center for the Arts

The writing is on the wall

The Mission

The Mission is the strangest of places.

While it seems all of San Francisco is banging on about how amazing this area is, to visit it during the day you'd wonder why. Admittedly, there's a big artist community here and great examples of murals and Victoriana, but on the surface it only seems to offer a bunch of low-rent junk shops, ethnic food-stores, taquerias and a none-too-wholesome-looking scene around the BART at 16th Street.

However, by night the seedier side of the area seems to disappear, or at least is blanketed by darkness – but always be on your guard – and the yuppies hit the streets to chow'n'sup at what are becoming the most fashionable restaurants and bars in an increasingly gentrified suburb. And if the Castro is home to gay men, the Mission is fast establishing itself as an area for a burgeoning lesbian scene.

That's not to say that there's nothing of interest sightseeing-wise in the Mission. It is in fact the oldest neighbourhood in San Francisco, inhabited by the Spanish initially, though it seems that every nationality has passed through this place at some point.

A DAY OUT

Essentially, you can do the Mission in an afternoon or less, or en route to the Castro, though if you're in the city for a limited time only, you might want to bypass it altogether – except for maybe an evening meal.

To best experience it, it's worth checking out the area between Dolores and Mission Streets from 16th Street down, even if some of it is residential. Get the BART here to 16th Street, which is good for soaking up the general 'atmosphere' of the area, though Mission Street is the main, if decrepit, thoroughfare, which caters to its poorer residents, hence its cheap supermarkets, junk stores, moneylenders and general rattiness. Valencia Street, towards Market Street, however, is much more palatable, with a whole bunch of cool cafés and restaurants.

In terms of sightseeing attractions, head three blocks east to Church Street to check out the area's main attraction, the blank white church, Mission Dolores. Inside the Mission check out the gilded altarpiece, ceramic mural and tiny museum, though you might be more interested to know it's the location from which Kim Novak famously plummets in the Hitchcock film *Vertigo*.

Next door is a more ornate basilica, although inside it holds nothing of real interest.

Nearby is Mission Dolores Park where you can check out a blinding view of San Francisco and the Bay. Loads of gay women live in the

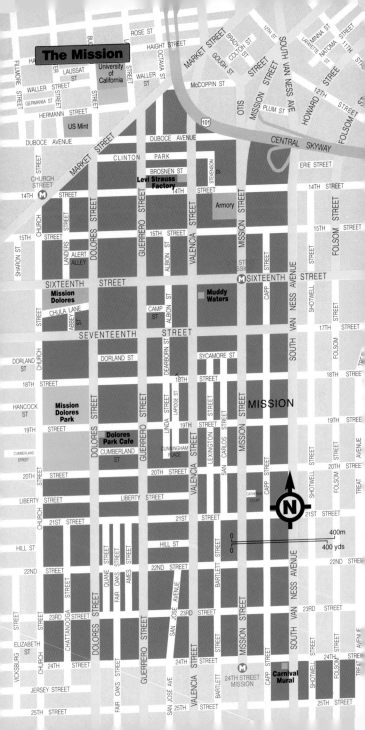

area, and when it's sunny this is where you can catch them strutting
their stuff on 'Dolores Beach', which also pulls in gay men from the
nearby Castro. Alternatively, the Dolores Park Café, though a real local
eaterie, also seems to be a popular lesbian hangout.

Continue much further south and you'll discover plenty of untouched
but quaint Victoriana between 19th and 24th Streets, though stand-out
examples nest on Liberty Street between 20th and 21st Streets.

Meanwhile, if you've dug the many murals in the Mission, you'll
definitely want to check the area's particularly excellent examples on 24th
Street. Carlos Santana is immortalised alongside images of the city's diverse
population in the Carnival Mural at South Van Ness Avenue, while further
down 24th, you'll discover a slew of examples known as Balmy Alley.

☕ Out to Lunch

Foodwise, the Mission really comes alive at
night, when you'll be spoilt for choice, though
the specialities here are Mexican *taquerias* and
trendy cuisine aimed at the yuppies in the
district. During the day, the café **Muddy
Waters** (521 Valencia Street at 16th Street) is a
good stop-off point, however, as it's away from
all the grunginess, even if it is a little shabby
itself, and it's also not too far from the
sightseeing attraction Mission Dolores. It's an
airy, open-plan brick-walled local joint
favoured by neighbourhood folk, with a few
tables and chairs outside. Offering a nice array
of teas, coffees, bagels, cakes and cookies, it's
a great place to chill and check out those
funky Mission folk.

Mural of Carlos
Santana and co.

MISSION DOLORES
ℹ️ 3221 Dolores Street
at 16th Street
✆ 415-621-8203
Ⓜ️ BART 16th Street;
Muni Metro F, J, K, L, M;
bus 22, 24
🕐 9am–4pm daily
💲 $2

The Mission District's
only real sightseeing
attraction, Mission
Dolores is the oldest
standing structure in
the city, dating from
1791.

OUTLINES

BALMY ALLEY
ℹ️ Off 24th Street,
between Treat and Harrison
Streets
Ⓜ️ BART 24th Street; bus
12, 48

A street showcasing
the city's penchant for
murals – even if some
of the residents are
now kinda resistant.

CARNIVAL MURAL
ℹ️ South Van Ness at
24th Street
Ⓜ️ BART 24th Street; bus
14, 48, 49

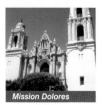
Mission Dolores

MISSION DOLORES PARK
ℹ️ At 18th, 20th, Church
and Dolores Streets
Ⓜ️ Muni Metro J;
bus 33

A large open space
popular with gay
gentlemen and lady
lesbians of the area.
Great views – in
every sense.

War Memorial Opera House

Civic Center, Hayes Valley and the Central Neighbourhoods

Civic Center, as the name implies, is where the city's official municipal buildings are situated. Though this might sound dull, the area is designed on a grand scale, with impressive boulevards and manicured lawns.

It's an architectural delight, with turn-of-the-20th-century Beaux-Arts buildings that are also home to many of the city's arts and performance centres. It should take you anything from a half-an-hour to a morning to cover, depending on how interested you are.

Nearby, the surprisingly flat Hayes Valley used to be where hookers and hustlers would hang out. That all changed after the 1989 earthquake, when this area began to morph into something much more funky. It's now a fashionable and promising little enclave, filled with eclectic stores, cafés and restaurants, definitely worth checking out if you're in the area.

Its main drag, Hayes Street, leads to Alamo Square, which is overlooked by one of the city's most photographed views of the city, as on the east side sit six picture-perfect examples of Victorian architecture.

A DAY OUT

Your first – and potentially, only – stop-off in Civic Center has to be the magnificent, if imposing, City Hall with its vast rotunda, the area's centrepiece. Take a photo, even if you're not going to have a look inside, which you can do for free.

Explore the following highlights in the area as you see fit. Across the green Civic Center Plaza is the Main Library with its grand five-storey atrium and grand staircase, which houses the Gay and Lesbian Center and from 2002 is to be home to the Asian Art Museum, formerly situated in Golden Gate Park.

Across Grove Street sits the Bill Graham Civic Auditorium, one of the city's most prominent performance venues, also in the Beaux-Arts style. Wander west and you'll discover the War Memorial Opera House on Van Ness Avenue, which is home to the San Francisco Opera. The nearby Veterans' Building contains the Herbst Theater, while the Louise M. Davies Symphony Hall, with its curved glass front, is where the San Francisco Symphony Orchestra play.

A stone's throw west from Civic Center and you're on a shabby-chic San Fran shopping stretch called Hayes Street (hence the name Hayes Valley),

Civic Center, Pacific Heights and the Central Neighbourhoods

TAYLOR STREET
ELLIS STREET
STREET
STREET
EDDY STREET
TURK STREET
Golden Gate Theater
GOLDEN GATE AVENUE
Law College
LEAVENWORTH STREET
HYDE STREET
STREET
Main Library (Asian Art Museum and Gay & Lesbian Center)
Orpheum Theater
United Nations Plaza
CIVIC CENTER
6TH STREET
JESSIE ST
STREET
MARKET STREET
STEVENSON ST
MISSION ST
SEVENTH STREET
JESSIE ST
MISSION STREET
Greyhound Terminal
LANGTON ST
RAUSCH ST
SUMNER ST
CLEMENTINA
MINNA
STREET
TEHAMA
HOWARD STREET
NATOMA
EIGHTH STREET
FOLSOM STREET
NINTH STREET
WASHBURN ST
GRACE ST
DORE
TENTH STREET
MINNA STREET
MA STREET
11TH STREET
LARKIN STREET
McALLISTER STREET
Brooks Hall (underground)
LARKIN STREET
Civic Center Plaza
Bill Graham Civic Auditorium
MARKET STREET
POLK STREET
EDDY STREET
WILLOW STREET
VAN NESS AVENUE
STREET
Pioneer Hall
VE STREET
City Hall
GRO
POLK STREET
HAYES STREET
VAN NESS AVENUE
SOUTH VAN NESS
VAN NESS
400m
400 yds

N

MISSION STREET
12TH STREET
LAF
BRADY
STEVENSON STREET
MARKET STREET
OCTAVIA STREET

TURK STREET
Jefferson Square
GOLDEN GATE AVENUE
FRANKLIN STREET
Veteran's Building (Herbst Theater)
War Memorial Opera House
Louise M. Davies Symphony Hall
Gimme Shoes
FRANKLIN STREET

Hayward Playground
McALLISTER STREET
FULTON STREET
GOUGH STREET
GOUGH STREET
HICKORY STREET
OAK STREET
LILY STREET
PAGE STREET
ROSE STREET
ST

GOUGH S
AVENUE
Western Addition Cultural Center
GROVE STREET
IVY STREET
Nomads
HAYES STREET
LINDEN STREET
Alabaster
FELL STREET
LAGUNA STREET
BUCHANAN ST
ROSE ST
HAIGHT STREET

LAGUNA STREET
McALLISTER STREET
FULTON STREET
IY STREET
BUCHANAN STREET
HAYES STREET
LINDEN STREET
HICKORY STREET
FELL STREET
LILY STREET
PAGE STREET
OAK STREET

EDDY STREET
WEBSTER STREET
CIVIC CENTER
WEBSTER STREET
BUCHANAN STREET
EBSTER STREET
HAIGHT STREET

Pacific Coast Hospital
WESTERN ADDITION
FILLMORE STREET
FILLMORE STREET
McALLISTER STREET
VALLEY
Postcard Row
HAYES VALLEY
FILLMORE STREET
OAK STREET
PAGE STREET

TURK STREET
STEINER STREET
GOLDEN GATE AVENUE
FULTON STREET
GROVE STREET
STEINER STREET
HAYES STREET
STEINER STREET

EDDY STREET
Kimball
WESTERN ADDITION
SCOTT STREET
TURK STREET
Alamo Square
FULTON STREET
GROVE ST
HAYES STREET
FELL STREET
OAK STREET
SCOTT STREET

PIERCE STREET
PIERCE STREET
PAGE STREET
HAIGHT STREET
INER STREET

which offers you yet another opportunity to flex your credit card as it features a funky mix of cool clothes stores and sexy brasseries. Special mention goes to footwear outlet Gimme Shoes, urban outfitters Nomads, and the exquisite antique housewares of Alabaster.

Continue west along Hayes Street and into what becomes a typical San Fran residential area, and in about 20 minutes or so you'll arrive at Alamo Square. A pretty if hilly little square which features a tennis court and playground, it's nevertheless famous for its pastel-shaded Postcard Row.

Alamo Square 'the Painted Ladies'

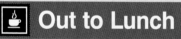

Out to Lunch

While Civic Center won't offer you much in the way of culinary delights, there's a mighty fine selection of cafés and lunch venues a couple of blocks away towards trendy Hayes Valley. **Citizen Cake** (399 Grove Street; open 7am–10pm Tues–Fri; 9am–10pm Sat–Sun; closed Mon) offers substantial main meals, though the real emphasis is on its bakery and pâtisseries. It might be small, and caters mainly to a takeaway crowd, but **Arlequin** (384 Hayes Street; open 8am–8pm Mon–Sat; noon–6pm Sun) has an eclectic menu featuring avocado salad, Albacore tuna sandwiches and grilled mushrooms on Levain bread. Check out the beautiful Amphora wine company next door.

OUTLINES

ALABASTER
🛈 597 Hayes Street at Laguna Street
📞 415-558-0482
www.alabastersf.com
🚌 Bus 16AX, 21, 22
🕐 11am–6pm Tues–Sat; noon–5pm Sun; closed Mon

Fancy-schmancy antiques and artwares store in the Hayes Valley.

ALAMO SQUARE
🛈 Between Scott and Steiner Streets at Fulton and Hayes Streets

Fantastic views down Hayes Valley to City Hall, but this hilly green space is most notable for its 'Six Sisters' Queen Anne-style houses, otherwise known as Postcard Row.

BILL GRAHAM CIVIC AUDITORIUM
🛈 99 Grove Street at Polk Street
📞 415-974-4060
🚇 BART Civic Center; Muni Metro F, J, K, L, M, N; bus 5, 9, 16AX, 21, 26, 47, 49

Named after a local rock promoter, this is a Beaux-Arts beauty and the city's most prominent performance venue.

CITY HALL
🛈 1 Dr Carlton B Goodlett Place, between Van Ness Avenue and Polk Street
📞 415-554-4000
🚌 Bus 5, 21
🕐 8am–8pm Mon–Fri; noon–4pm Sat; closed Sun
🎟 Free

The jewel in the crown of the Beaux-Arts Civic Center, City Hall houses the Mayor's office, the Board of Supervisors,

Striking modern architecture contrasts with older buildings

chamber and local government offices as well as rolling exhibitions.

GIMME SHOES

🛈 416 Hayes Street at Gough Street

🌐 415-434-9242

🚍 Bus 21

🕒 11am–6pm Mon–Sat; 11am–6pm Sun

Designer shoe outlet with a nice range in trainers.

LOUISE M. DAVIES SYMPHONY HALL

🛈 201 Van Ness Avenue at Grove Street

🌐 415-552-8338

🚇 BART Civic Center; Muni Metro F, J, K, L, M, N; bus 5, 9, 16AX, 21, 26, 47, 49

Named after the philanthropist who coughed up a hefty portion of the cost, this loved and loathed 1980s building is home to the San Francisco Symphony Orchestra.

NOMADS

🛈 556 Hayes Street, between Gough and Octavia Streets

🌐 415-864-5697

🚍 Bus 16AX, 21, 22

🕒 11am–7pm Tues–Sat; 11pm–6pm Sun–Mon

Cool'n'sexy urban B-boy store.

The flag flies across the city

SAN FRANCISCO MAIN LIBRARY

🛈 100 Larkin Street at Grove Street

🌐 415-557-4400 http://sfpl.lib.ca.us

🚇 BART Civic Center; Muni Metro F, J, K, L, M, N; bus 5, 9, 16AX, 21, 26, 47, 49

🕒 10am–6pm Mon and Sat; 9am–8pm Tues–Thu; noon–6pm Fri; noon–5pm Sun

Built around a monumental staircase, this 1917 building features African-American, Asian and Gay and Lesbian centres, plus a great wealth of historic material.

VETERANS' BUILDING

🛈 401 Van Ness Avenue at McAllister Street

🌐 415-621-6600

🚇 BART Civic Center; Muni Metro F, J, K, L, M, N; bus 5, 9, 16AX, 21, 26, 47, 49

Although it looks like the War Memorial Opera House, don't be fooled – this one's the home of the Herbst Theatre.

WAR MEMORIAL OPERA HOUSE

🛈 455 Franklin Street, between Grove and Fulton Streets

🌐 415-621-6600

🚇 BART Civic Center; Muni Metro F, J, K, L, M, N; bus 5, 9, 16AX, 21, 26, 47, 49

🕒 10am–6pm Mon–Sat

If opera's the thing that lights your candle, here's San Francisco's number one venue.

The Peace Pagoda in Japantown

Japantown, Pacific Heights and Cow Hollow

Japantown is exactly that, a section of San Francisco catering to the approximately 12,000 citizens of Japanese descent. The Japan Center is based here. But the area is neither the hi-tech nor ancient replica of a Japanese metropolis you might expect.

Pacific Heights is the most desirable residential area in San Francisco, so no prizes for guessing that it's also the most expensive. The reason for all the interest? The houses. Pacific Heights has beautiful and well-maintained Victorian pads like nowhere else in the city, and it's good to while away hours just wandering around. Cow Hollow is named after the lush pasture it once was. At its centre is Union Street, filled with Victorian homes converted into shops and cute cafés. While it offers boutique shopping for ladies who lunch, that's not to say that you won't find something for you here.

A DAY OUT

Get the 38 bus along the Geary Expressway and get off at Gough Street if you want to check out the relatively modern St Mary's Cathedral. Simple inside, outside it's either an impressive, domineering white structure or a supersize kitchen appliance – take your pick. Head a couple of blocks east to check out the Japan Center at the heart of Japantown. Built in 1968, it's a showcase for Japanese culture. Outside you'll discover the Peace Plaza Garden, which is overlooked by the concrete Peace Pagoda, donated by Japan. Explore the surrounding streets and you'll find a selection of Japanese and Korean restaurants.

Head north into Pacific Heights. At Washington Street, between Fillmore and Webster and east of hilltop park Alta Plaza, you'll find a block of Victorian houses. Continue along Washington to the quiet Lafayette Park for a rest, or check out the impressive baroque Spreckels Mansion.

If you wish to have a further gander at quintessential Victoriana, make a detour east for either the Octagon House or the Haas–Lilienthal House. Surprisingly, neither are as pretty as you'd expect, with the latter's dark exterior reminiscent of Anthony Perkins' house in *Psycho*.

Wanna shop? Head back west to Fillmore Street, Pacific Heights' main shopping drag. It seems to specialise in cutesy stores offering cards, beads and scented candles, but if you continue along it you'll get to the superior shopping experience of Union Street, between Steiner and Gough Streets. Union offers a stretch of chi-chi fashions, galleries, jewellers and interior design. It's definitely worth an amble if you're around, though it's hardly a true reflection of what San Francisco is really about. Armani Exchange and Nida supply designer menswear, while Loft is a homeware store.

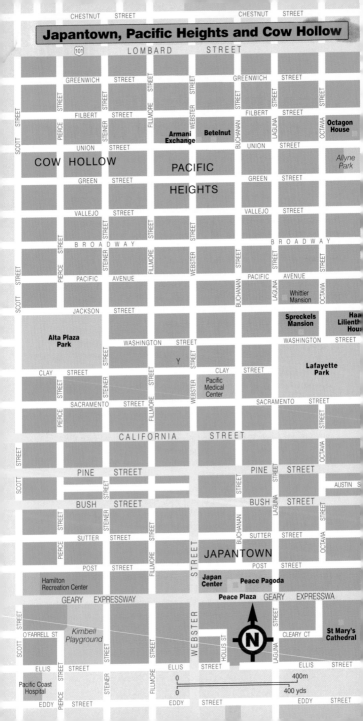

Japantown, Pacific Heights and Cow Hollow

CHESTNUT STREET · CHESTNUT STREET

[101] · LOMBARD STREET

GREENWICH STREET · GREENWICH STREET

FILBERT STREET · FILBERT STREET

Armani Exchange · **Betelnut** · **Octagon House**

UNION STREET · UNION STREET

COW HOLLOW · PACIFIC · Allyne Park

GREEN STREET · HEIGHTS · GREEN STREET

VALLEJO STREET · VALLEJO STREET

BROADWAY · BROADWAY

PACIFIC AVENUE · PACIFIC AVENUE

Whittier Mansion

JACKSON STREET · **Spreckels Mansion** · **Haa Lilienth Hous**

Alta Plaza Park · WASHINGTON STREET · WASHINGTON STREET

Lafayette Park

CLAY STREET · CLAY STREET

Pacific Medical Center

SACRAMENTO STREET · SACRAMENTO STREET

CALIFORNIA STREET

PINE STREET · PINE STREET

AUSTIN S

BUSH STREET · BUSH STREET

SUTTER STREET · SUTTER STREET

POST STREET · **JAPANTOWN** · POST STREET

Hamilton Recreation Center · **Japan Center** · **Peace Pagoda**

Peace Plaza · GEARY EXPRESSWA

GEARY EXPRESSWAY

O'FARRELL ST · *Kimbell Playground* · CLEARY CT · **St Mary's Cathedral**

ELLIS STREET · ELLIS STREET · ELLIS STREET

Pacific Coast Hospital

0 _____ 400m
0 _____ 400 yds

EDDY STREET · EDDY STREET · EDDY STREET

SCOTT STREET · PIERCE STREET · STEINER STREET · FILLMORE STREET · WEBSTER STREET · BUCHANAN STREET · LAGUNA STREET · OCTAVIA STREET · HOLLIS ST

Out to Lunch

You can pick up top-quality *sushi* and Japanese food all across San Francisco, so you don't need to make a special pilgrimage to Japantown especially for it – though if you do, there are loads of restaurants which will offer it to you on a conveyor belt, literally. However, you won't be disappointed if you do make a special detour for lunch at **Betelnut** (2030 Union Street; *see p. 94*), as it delivers top-quality and fresh-tasting Asian classics in stylish surroundings.

OUTLINES

ALTA PLAZA PARK
ℹ️ Between Scott and Steiner Streets
🚍 Bus 3, 12

Green space with great views, right in the centre of Pacific Heights.

ARMANI EXCHANGE
ℹ️ 2090 Union Street at Webster Street
☎️ 415-749-0891
🚍 Bus 22, 41, 45
🕒 10am–8pm Mon–Sat; 11am–6pm Sun

Cheap diffusion range in small stylish store for male and female Armani devotees.

HAAS-LILIENTHAL HOUSE
ℹ️ 2007 Franklin Street at Washington Street
☎️ 415-441-3004
🚍 BART Civic Center; bus 12, 27, 42, 49
🕒 Noon–3pm Wed; 11am–4pm Sun

Once a modest upper middle-class home, this revered Queen Anne-style mansion with original furniture, now a museum, is one of the last of these types of building not destroyed by earthquake or fire.

JAPAN CENTER, PEACE PLAZA AND PEACE PAGODA
ℹ️ 1625 Post Street, between Geary, Laguna and Fillmore Streets
☎️ 415-922-6776
🚍 Bus 2, 3, 4, 38

The heart of the Japanese Community for the past century.

LAFAYETTE PARK
ℹ️ Between Laguna and Gough Streets
🚍 Bus 1, 12

The quiet hilltop gardens, smelling of eucalyptus and pine, give great views of the local Victoriana in Pacific Heights.

OCTAGON HOUSE
ℹ️ 2645 Gough Street
🚍 Bus 41, 45
🕒 Noon–3pm 2nd Sun, 2nd and 4th Thu
🎟️ Free

Built in 1861, Octagon House now has a small collection of arts and historic documents.

ST MARY'S CATHEDRAL
ℹ️ 1111 Gough Street
☎️ 415-567-2020
🚍 Bus 31, 38
🕒 6.45am–4.30pm Mon–Fri; 6.45am–6.30pm Sat; 7.15am–4.45pm Sun

This 1971 religious masterpiece is both loved and loathed.

SPRECKELS MANSION
ℹ️ 2080 Washington Street (not open to public)
🚍 Bus 1, 12

This 1912 Beaux-Arts building was built by the extravagant Spreckels couple.

Leg it around Haight Ashbury

Haight Ashbury

In the Victorian era, the Haight (pronounced 'hate') was a popular weekend resort. While its architecture lives on, it's much more famous for being a hippie hangout during the flower children's 1960s heyday. Things might not seem to have changed much, as it's still pretty ropey around the edges, if not plain dirty. This area still nurtures an 'alternative' culture, which finds its home in a hotch-potch collection of shops, cafés, clubs restaurants and bars along Haight Street. The area is best for shopping, and if you're sporting a) unusual facial hair; b) a floor-length, purple-mirror encrusted tassled skirt; c) a piercing other than in your ear; d) an oversize skatey T-shirt; e) all of the above, chances are you'll find something for you in the Haight. For everyone else, there's always the branch of GAP.

A DAY OUT

If you're approaching Haight Street on foot from downtown, you might be persuaded to check out the Lower Haight, which runs from Webster to Scott Streets. It's been resistant to gentrification and is home only to degenerate-looking record shacks, eateries, street vendors selling junk and a skatey-looking scene. However, Costumes on Haight is a tiny, jam-packed jewel box of a secondhand store.

You might want to start your visit at the more appealing Buena Vista Park, which veers up steeply from Haight Street and is kinda wild in comparison to other San Fran green spots. Get buses 6, 7, 66 or 71 here.

Continue west and the Haight proper starts up after Central Avenue and continues to Stanyan Street, the border of Golden Gate Park. Two blocks north runs the Pan-handle in parallel, an eight-block stretch of parkland, precursor to Golden Gate Park.

Before you engage in the shopping, you might want to check out an example of a Queen Anne-style house. The Richard

Get suited and booted

Spreckels Mansion is on the border of Buena Vista Park south of Haight,. while 1220 Masonic Avenue is another example of cutesy Victoriana further west.

Continue along Haight to shop, shop, shop along this stretch of stores. There are some cool outlets: Stussy's trademark skatewear can be found here, The Booksmith is just that, and Shoe Biz and Villains offer a selection of mid-price to spendy shoes and clothing. Special mention has to go, however, to the breathtaking Amoeba Music, which will fulfil all of your music needs. In an area packed to the gills with secondhand stores, Wasteland is the city's most famous and worth a gander. Finally, if you're thinking of getting a tattoo done, boy, are you in the right area. Ignore the rest, the best are to be found in the world-famous Mom's Body Shop.

Out to Lunch

When it comes to eating in Haight Ashbury, it's a bit of a challenge to find something that caters to anyone with a little more style than the student-looking denizens around. Most places, you wouldn't even want to drop your napkin on the floor. However, **Grind Cafe** (783 Haight Street; open 7am–10pm daily) will give you decent enough coffee and hefty breakfasts (a shout out goes to the pancakes). The more discerning visitor might want to check out the **Magnolia Pub and Brewery** (1398 Haight Street; open 11am–11pm Mon–Fri; 10am–11pm Sat–Sun) for more than their ales. There are sandwiches for lunch, while entrées include a yummy mix of styles and tastes at a reasonable price.

OUTLINES

BUENA VISTA PARK

ℹ️ Between Central Avenue and Baker Streets

🚍 Bus 6, 7, 66, 71

At times overgrown, this park sprawls south of the Haight.

RICHARD SPRECKELS MANSION

ℹ️ 737 Buena Vista West, between Waller and Frederick Streets

🚍 Bus 6, 7, 37, 43, 66, 71

Built by millionaire Claus Spreckels in 1897, this Queen Anne house has been a recording studio and guesthouse. Not open to the public.

STUSSY

ℹ️ 1409 Haight Street

📞 415-701-7474

🚍 Muni Metro N; bus 6, 7, 33, 37, 43

🕐 11am–7pm Mon–Sat; 11am–6pm Sun

Experience the ultimate skatewear in the tiny but only Stussy store in San Francisco.

VILLAINS

ℹ️ 1672 Haight Street;

📞 415-626-5939

🚍 Muni Metro N; bus 6, 7, 33, 37, 43

🕐 11am–7pm daily

Three stores of menswear and womenswear ranging from street to chic.

The Art-Deco Castro Theater features a Mighty Wurlitzer Organ

The Castro and Twin Peaks

As a gay visitor, you can't visit San Francisco without checking into the Castro at some point, if only to dig the vibe.

Home to most of the gay and lesbian population of the city and always busy, its main drag is Castro Street, though make sure you don't miss Market, between Castro and Church Streets, as it's where you'll find a good selection of interesting little shops and restaurants. Whether you want to go sightseeing, have a drink, go cruising or party real hard, the Castro is where it's all at.

Meanwhile, the Twin Peaks provide an awesome view of the city. According to Indian legend, the two mountains were once twin daughters of an Indian chief, though the original Spanish name was Los Pechos de la Choca (The Breasts of the Indian Maiden). Whatever, it's a bit of hassle getting to, but it's more than worth it on a clear day, when you can get a different view of the city.

A DAY OUT

Getting off at the Muni Metro stop, you'll find yourself at a crossroads. From here want to check out Castro Street ahead and Market Street to your left in what looks like a typical San Francisco, if villagey, neighbourhood, but for the rainbow flags hanging from windows and painted on street posts.

First point of call on Castro Street should be the Castro Theater, though en route take a look at the glass-fronted Twin Peaks on your left, the area's first gay bar. The Castro Theater is an ornate Art-Deco cinema which still features a Mighty Wurlitzer Organ that provides a mini-concert during intermissions. The theatre shows classic, international and gay films from a varied tradition.

Ahead you'll discover Harvey's, a Hard Rock Café-style bar and grill across the street from the site of Harvey Milk's old camera shop. He was the city's first openly-gay elected official, see page 10. Look above the Skin Zone for a mural of the legend himself.

When it comes to shopping, take a look at Rolo for homie menswear, Does Your Mother/Father Know? and Rock Hard for typical gay schmutter, knick-knacks and toys, while A Different Light will satisfy your literary needs.

Go back to the Muni Metro stop and head east along busy Market Street towards Church Street. The Names Project is where you can see the AIDS quilt. Each patch represents the work of someone who has lost a relative or friend to the disease. Along this stretch of Market, there is a

The Castro and Twin Peaks

bevy of interesting stores; another branch of Rolo for more discerning label queens, and the yummy organic store Harvest Market.

But while shops will amuse, it's the local talent which will totally distract you, and there are a couple of prime locations where you can people-watch… OK, cruise. The Café and Metro both have balconies, the former turning into a club later on in the evening. However, most bars open at noon and you should find one to suit your particular tastes. Much like the rest of San Fran, step away from the stores in the Castro and you'll discover pastel-coloured, Victoriana-lined residential streets.

Want to check out that view from Twin Peaks? Bus 36 or bus 37 from Muni Metro are by far the easiest ways to get there, though you might want to bike it if you're feeling athletic. However you get there, you'll get a breathtaking view diagonally along Market to Downtown. On a good day, you'll even be able to see Berkeley, and at night the vista glitters like a dream.

Out to Lunch

There are lots of outdoor cafés and restaurants in the neighbourhood, all, unsurprisingly, with an obviously gay atmosphere. For a real local experience, check out **Café Flore** (2298 Market Street; tel 415-621-8579; *see p. 97*), which is legendary as much for its home-cooked meals, breads, cakes and pastries as for its clientèle. If it's packed to the gills, why not try the nearby **Baghdad Cafe** (*see p. 102*) or even better, bag yourself a takeout from **Harvest Market** (2285 Market Street; open 8.30am– 11pm daily) and eat on one of the rafters outside?

OUTLINES

THE CAFE

🛈 2367 Market Street

📞 415-861-3846

🚇 Muni Metro F, K, L, M; bus 35, 37

🕐 1pm–2am daily

Relax on the balcony during the day, get down on the dance-floor at night.

CASTRO THEATER

🛈 429 Castro Street

📞 415-621-6120

🚇 Muni Metro F, K, L, M; bus 24, 35, 37

Relive the 1920s and experience the best in gay movies at this landmark cinema.

THE NAMES PROJECT

🛈 2362A Market Street

📞 415-863-1966

🚇 Muni Metro F, J, K, L, M; bus 22, 33, 37

🕐 noon–5pm Mon–Fri

Made up of over 60,000 individual panels, the AIDS Memorial Quilt was started in 1987 and is an emotional testament to everyone who has died of AIDS.

TWIN PEAKS

🛈 Twin Peaks Boulevard, between Glenview Drive and Woodside Avenue

🚇 Bus 36, 37

Get a different view of the city from this double-peaked mountain at its south-west corner.

A bird's eye view of the bridge

Presidio and Golden Gate Bridge

The Presidio is an expansive green sprawl which connects the Marina District to the Richmond District in the north of the city. Once a military outpost, it became a national park in 1993.

It is home to the Palace of Fine Arts, a pet cemetery (yes, really!), a golf course, beaches (including a nudist stretch), *faux* colonial buildings, thickets and untamed open spaces. It also provides the jumping-off point for one end of the Golden Gate Bridge. It is a great place for hiking, cycling and – on a good day – going to the beach within city limits.

The Golden Gate Bridge is a must-see, though you will already be very familiar with it, as it features on almost every postcard you might send from San Francisco.

A DAY OUT

To cover the Presidio in any kind of detail, you'll really want to use a car, public transport or a guided tour option – at least to drop you off in a relevant spot. The freeways that run through it can be more than a little off-putting to pedestrians, though it's possible to make light sorties into the area from West Pacific Avenue or Lyon Street.

Its north-eastern corner is walkable, however. Get to the Exploratorium in the Palace of Fine Arts, built in 1915 to celebrate the Panama Pacific International Exhibition, via the 28 or 43 bus. Take a look at the Greco-Romanesque rotunda beside the lake. If you're here for arts, fine or otherwise, you're going to be disappointed. The Exploratorium is a massive, hands-on science museum covering technology, nature and art. It will thrill you if you're a big kid, and amuse you even if you're not. Don't miss the section which shows you how Hollywood works its magic. This is California, after all.

If you're on foot, you *love* walking and you're not faint-hearted, head south along Lyon to Green, where you'll discover the Lyon Street Steps, an almost never-ending but stylish stone staircase which affords great views of Alcatraz, the Palace of Fine Arts and the Golden Gate Bridge.

From now on you might want to pick up your wheels. Head east from the Palace of Fine Arts and you'll discover Crissy Field, part green space, part reclaimed army area, where you can take a decent, hour-long walk in what is a popular area for cyclists and joggers. Opposite stands the white wooden Presidio Museum, where you can check out military and political Californian history.

Travel along Freeway 101 – the 28 or 76 bus will take you – past the Military Cemetery to Golden Gate Bridge, which is guarded by brick

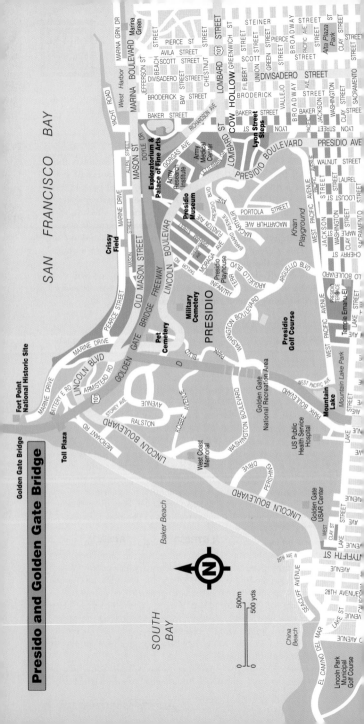

Presido and Golden Gate Bridge

Golden Gate Bridge

SAN FRANCISCO BAY

SOUTH BAY

Fort Point National Historic Site

Toll Plaza

Baker Beach

China Beach

MARINE DRIVE

BATTERY E RD

LINCOLN BLVD

MERCHANT RD

ARMISTEAD RD

PEARCE STREET

GOLDEN GATE BRIDGE FREEWAY

OLD MASON STREET

MASON ST

MARINE DRIVE

ALLEN STREET

DOYLE DR

GORGAS AVE

RICHARDSON AVE

LYON ST

LOMBARD ST

BAKER STREET

BRODERICK STREET

BAY STREET

CHESTNUT STREET

DIVISADERO STREET

BRODERICK

SCOTT STREET

AVILA STREET

PIERCE ST

BEACH STREET

JEFFERSON STREET

JEFFERSON ST

West Harbor

West Marina

MARINA GRN DR

MARINA Marina Green

MARINA BOULEVARD

STEINER STREET

BROADWAY

PACIFIC AVE

Alta Plaza Park

CLAY STREET

LOMBARD STREET

GREENWICH ST

FILBERT STREET

UNION STREET

GREEN STREET

PIERCE STREET

SCOTT STREET

COW HOLLOW

DIVISADERO STREET

VALLEJO STREET

BROADWAY

WASHINGTON STREET

JACKSON STREET

CLAY STREET

SACRAMENTO

SACRAMENTO

BAKER STREET

LYON STREET

Lyon Street Steps

PRESIDIO BOULEVARD

PRESIDIO AVE

WALNUT STREET

LAUREL STREET

LOCUST ST

MAPLE STREET

SPRUCE ST

CHERRY ST

ARGUELLO BLVD

PALM AVE

JACKSON STREET

WEST PACIFIC AVENUE

WASHINGTON

CLAY ST

PRESIDIO TERRACE

Exploratorium & Palace of Fine Arts

Army Medical Center

Army Research Institute

Presidio Museum

PORTOLA STREET

FUNSTON AVE

PRESIDIO BLVD

MORAGA AVE

MACARTHUR AVE

BERNARD AVE

ARGUELLO BLVD

INFANTRY

TAYLOR RD

MORAGA AVE

Presidio Playhouse

Khan Playground

Crissy Field

LINCOLN BOULEVARD

MISSION STREET

STOREY AVE

KOBBE AVENUE

RALSTON

LINCOLN BOULEVARD

WASHINGTON BOULEVARD

PARK BOULEVARD

MCDOWELL AVE

PERSHING DRIVE

Military Cemetery

Pet Cemetery

PRESIDIO

Golden Gate National Recreation Area

Presidio Golf Course

Temple Emanu-El

LAKE STREET

Mountain Lake

Mountain Lake Park

WEST PACIFIC AVE

West Coast Memorial

US Public Health Service Hospital

Golden Gate USAR Center

Golden Gate National Recreation Area

SEACLIFF AVENUE

EL CAMINO DEL MAR

Lincoln Park Municipal Golf Course

28TH AVENUE N

28TH AVENUE

LAKE STREET

CLAY ST

LAKE STREET

TWELFTH ST

AVENUE

N

500m
500 yds
0

fortress Fort Point. There are parking spaces at either end, though the best way to experience the crossing is either by foot or bicycle.

From the Golden Gate Bridge, head south along Lincoln Boulevard (on the 29 bus) and you come to Baker Beach, the best of the city's beaches. You can also reach it via Marine Drive, a waterfront roadway. The beach offers sunbathing, naked and otherwise, but if you want to keep relatively covered up, head to the south end of the beach.

If you want to head inland, do so off the southern border of the Presidio, a block north of Lake Street. Here's where you can check out acres of green space, a manicured golf course, the pretty Mountain Lake and that pet cemetery, once used to bury army dogs but now the resting place for family pets.

Out to Lunch

Difficult, this one. There is a small café in the Exploratorium, but with all those kids running around it's hardly likely to be the greatest experience for you, and when it comes to the Presidio, things don't get much better. Considering that it's mostly open space, believe it to be a culinary wasteland too. Make sure you're fed and watered before setting out, or – and I'm not joking here – take a packed lunch.

OUTLINES

EXPLORATORIUM

- 3601 Lyon Street
- 415-397-5673
- www.exploratorium.edu
- Bus 28, 30, 30X, 76
- Labor Day– Memorial Day 10am–5pm Tues–Sun; 10am–9pm Wed; Memorial Day–Labor Day 10am– 6pm Mon– Tues and Thu– Sun; 10am–9pm Wed
- $9

A vast warehouse of a museum with hands-on interactive displays that teach you about sciences, the senses and much, much more.

GOLDEN GATE BRIDGE

- Access from the Toll Plaza at the Presidio
- Bus 10, 20, 28
- $3 for vehicles

San Francisco's most famous landmark – well worth it.

LYON STREET STEPS

- Lyon Street, between Green and Broadway Streets
- Bus 41, 45

Steep, stylish stone steps, which run along the barren eastern edge of the Presidio.

PALACE OF FINE ARTS

- 3301 Lyon Street
- 415-563-6504
- Bus 28, 30, 30X, 76
- 6am–9pm daily

This beautiful rotunda overlooks a serene lake.

PRESIDIO MUSEUM

- Funston Avenue and Lincoln Boulevard
- 415-561-4331
- Bus 28, 29, 76
- 10am–4pm Wed–Sun

Once the Presidio hospital, now a military memorabilia museum.

Find tranquility in the Japanese Tea Garden

Golden Gate Park and California Academy of Sciences

Well planned with shrubs and bushes to ensure there's colour all year round, Golden Gate Park shines brightest in the summer, when all of San Francisco seems to converge here to chill out, go jogging, play sports, check out the museums and perform. Since its evolution under the guidance of landscape maestro William Hammond Hall in 1871, it's been home to many events such as rock concerts and festivals, while also providing vital shelter for the homeless and earthquake victims.

The main attractions here are of a museum and garden nature, though the park also has a herd of bison, believe it or not.

A DAY OUT

Golden Gate Park covers 1013 acres of land of green space, woods and landscaped gardens. A good way to see it is by bike. Check out Golden Gate Park Cyclery (1749 Waller Street; tel 415-221-3777). Start at John F. Kennedy Drive at Stanyan Street and follow it east, checking out the McLaren Lodge on your right. The National AIDS Memorial Grove isn't the easiest place to find, but is a quiet and restful spot at the foot of a hill with inscriptions in the paving. Continue along John F. Kennedy Drive past the Lily Pond and the Conservatory of Flowers, and turn into Hagiwara Tea Garden Drive. Here's where you'll locate the Music Concourse, with fountains, benches and trees overlooked by the Spreckels Temple of Music, the venue for open-air concerts. On the right is the pale pink Spanish-looking complex featuring the De Young Museum (closed until 2005). Next door is the Japanese Tea Garden, an essential stop. Highlighting typical Japanese landscaping features like giant Buddhas and goldfish ponds, it's tiny but pretty and tranquil if not overrun by tourists.

Nearby sits the California Academy of Sciences, home to the Steinhart Aquarium, the Natural History Museum, the Morrison Planetarium and Laserium. The courtyard features its famous fountain, *Mating Whales*, and the buildings around offer a widely varied collection of subjects. You'll have to pay extra for the planetary experience, but the earthquake simulation, dinosaur displays, lifesize animal displays, fish tanks and other weird stuff you'll have never seen before will certainly fill an hour or so of your time.

The Strybing Arboretum is a living plant museum. It's an open space featuring ponds, paths and over 6000 plant species from around the world. Continue west and you'll discover Stow Lake, an artificial lake on which you can hire a paddleboat and look at the red and green Chinese

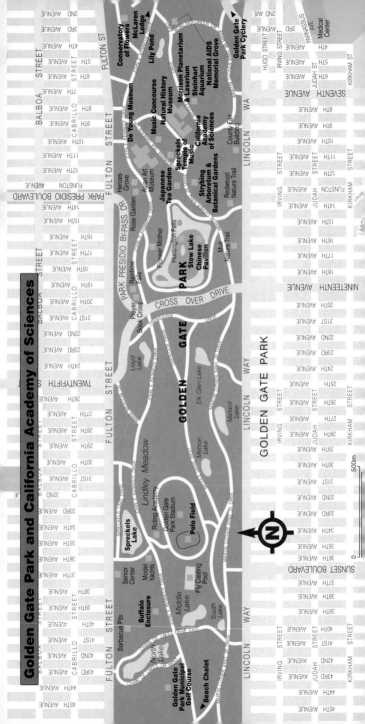

Golden Gate Park and California Academy of Sciences

Pavilion on shore, originally donated by San Francisco's sister city Taipei.

The further west you head, the more parklife gives way to sports arenas like polo fields and a golf course, however just past Spreckels Lake you can discover those buffalos for yourself! Continue even further west, and you'll find the 1920s Beach Chalet, which overlooks the Pacific Ocean. It opened as a restaurant and bathhouse back in 1925, and is the site of a Lucien Labaudt mural depicting life during the Great Depression.

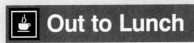

Out to Lunch

Choices of quality chow in Golden Gate Park are limited. Yes, the California Academy Of Sciences has an **Academy Café**, but it's more like a functional and straightforward canteen. Meanwhile, if you can hang out while you schlep the three miles to the other end of the park, you'll find the still-in-action and relatively cheap restaurant at the **Beach Chalet**. It is, however, usually packed with tourists. So the advice? Stop off somewhere yummy before you get here.

OUTLINES

BEACH CHALET
🛈 1000 Great Highway
📞 415-751-2766 (info);
415-386-8439 (restaurant)
🚍 Bus 5, 18
🕔 8am–6pm daily

This 1920s beach chalet is now a visitor centre, though you can still eat in the restaurant here.

CALIFORNIA ACADEMY OF SCIENCES
🛈 Music Concourse, Golden Gate Park
📞 415-750-7145
www.calacademy.org
🚍 Muni Metro N; bus 5, 16AX, 21, 44, 71
🕔 summer 9am–6pm daily; winter 10am–5pm daily 🎟 $8.50; $2.50 for the Planetarium

This interesting museum offers earth, air, water and space.

CONSERVATORY OF FLOWERS
🛈 John F. Kennedy Drive, Golden Gate Park
📞 415-641-7978
🚍 Bus 5, 21

Housing the largest collection of tropical plants in the world, at the time of writing it was closed for renovations.

JAPANESE TEA GARDEN
🛈 Music Concourse, Golden Gate Park
📞 415-668-0909
🚍 Muni Metro N; bus 5, 21, 44, 71
🕔 summer 8.30am–6pm daily; winter 8.30am–5pm
🎟 $3.50

A beautiful Japanese garden recreation.

STOW LAKE
🛈 Stow Lake Drive, Golden Gate Park
🚍 Bus 5, 28, 29
🕔 9am–5pm daily

Hire a paddleboat and drift around this peaceful artificial lake.

STRYBING ARBORETUM
🛈 9th Avenue and Lincoln Way
📞 415-661-1316
🚍 Muni Metro N; bus 5, 21, 44, 71
🕔 8am–4.30pm Mon–Fri; 10am–5pm Sat–Sun and holidays

A vast garden/ museum dedicated to plants, trees and shrubs from everywhere.

You'll go nuts about this shop

All Shopped Out

Admit it. As much as you're here to see the Golden Gate Bridge, you've also come to work your flexible friend to within an inch of his life. While San Francisco can't quite compete with New York or Los Angeles when it comes to the designer league, it does have all the necessary chains. The city, however, excels at the edgy, arty and eclectic – you might want to call it 'shabby chic'. If you're after quality secondhand clothes, Haight Ashbury is busting with thrift emporia, while Hayes Valley, Union Street and even the Castro have a good selection of trendy clothes outlets. If you're after funky knick-knacks or antiques, have a wander down Polk Street or Market Street, west of Van Ness Avenue. And the best thing about all this shopping? Hitting the various destinations will help you get a real handle on the city's landmarks and eclectic neighbourhoods.

Top of the Shops

American Rag

🛈 1305 Van Ness Avenue, between Bush and Sutter Streets
📞 415-474-5214
🚌 Bus 42, 47, 49, 76
🕙 10am–9pm Mon–Sat; noon–7pm Sun

The glorified freeway that is Van Ness Avenue would hardly seem like a first port of call for clothes shopping, as cheap furniture stores are the only outlets that seem to cluster there. American Rag, however, is a true find. This fantastic shop offers not only must-have brands for men and women, such as G-Star, Stussy, Paul Smith and Paul and Joe, but also a fine selection of top-end secondhand gear, from T-shirts to Levis, and from Hawaiian shirts to... well, you name it.

Amoeba Music

ℹ️ 1855 Haight Street
☎ 415-831-1200
www.amoebamusic.com
🚌 Bus 7, 33, 66
🕐 10.30am–10pm
Mon–Sat; 11am–9pm Sun

Music for all tastes

Amoeba is a musical hypermarket – it used to be a bowling alley, so you can imagine the size. Featuring old, new and used CDs, LPs, tapes, videos and posters, every genre is covered in full – electronica, techno, house, soul, rock, jazz or classical. They also buy, sell and trade. With in-store performances too, the question is not what are you after, but can you handle it.

City Lights

ℹ️ 261 Columbus Avenue
☎ 415-362 8193
🚌 Bus 9AX, 12, 15, 30X, 83
🕐 10am–midnight daily

City Lights looks like a real thrown-together bookshop. While it can't live up to the current super-bookstores like Borders, it more than makes up for it in authenticity. It can trace its history back to the Beat era, when it was founded by poet Lawrence Ferlinghetti, and if you want to soak up the atmosphere, or more importantly get your hands on an extensive range of fiction, here's where you should be heading. Fiction is divided by continent, and upstairs you can check out poetry and Beat writing, man.

Banana Republic

ℹ️ 256 Grant Avenue at Sutter Street
☎ 415-788-3087
www.bananarepublic.com
🕐 9.30am–8pm Mon–Sat; 11am–6pm Sun

A UK invasion by this popular chain is inevitable at some point, but until then you'll have to hotfoot it to America to get your hands on their upmarket but highly wearable GAP-alike goodies. And this flagship store just down the road from the Chinatown Gates houses affordable smart-casual T-shirts, shirts, trousers, suits and shoes in swish white surroundings. Search out a helpful personal shopper if you're really flashing cash. Classy homewares are worth a look too.

Chain store shopping

Crate and Barrel

🛈 55 Stockton Street
☎ 415-986-4000
www.crateandbarrel.com
🕐 10am–7pm Mon–Wed & Sat; 10am–8pm Thu–Fri; 11am–6pm Sun

No surprises for guessing that Crate and Barrel is an interiors store, and their new Union Square branch spreads over three expansive floors. Admittedly, it's part of a big old chain, and some of the furniture, featured on the top two floors, is kinda conservative. But these people really excel at the smaller pieces, with some pretty, sleek glass and clean white lines. Martha Stewart would be hugely impressed.

Harvest Market

🛈 2285 Market Street at Noe Street ☎ 415-626-0805 www.harvestranch.com 🕐 8.30am–11pm daily

Harvest Market is a fantastic organic deli-supermarket on Market in the Castro, which really puts to shame some of the sit-down eateries just around the block. Featuring a mouth-watering selection of fruit and veg and pre-packaged produce in a clean, stylish environment, Harvest Market also works a takeout trade with a deli counter and a cool, crunchy salad bar. Purchase, retire and enjoy on the low wooden benches outside. And oh yeah, if you've got a discerning pooch, there's even a basket of organic dog biscuits.

Gimme Shoes

❶ 416 Hayes Street **☎** 415-434-9242
Ⓜ Bus 21 **🕑** 11am–6pm Mon–Sat;
11am–6pm Sun

You don't have to have a Imelda
Marcos-like addiction to be blown
away by the shoe selection in the
Hayes Street branch of this top store.
The latest male and female footwear
lines from Dries Van Noten, Dirk
Bikkemberg, Samsonite, Prada, etc. are
presented simply in this wooden-fitted
shop – and that only seems to make
you want them more. There's even a
top-end range of trainers from Puma
and Adidas to covet.

Wasteland

❶ 1660 Haight Street **☎** 415-863-3150
Ⓜ Muni Metro N; bus
6, 7, 33, 37, 43 **🕑** 11am–7pm Sun–Thu;
11am–8pm Fri–Sat

Wasteland is legendary among
secondhand stores. A warehouse-like
space filled with goodies, if you can
wear it, you can probably find it here
– fur, polyester, cotton, vinyl, leather...
If you're after a pair of used cowboy
boots or brothel creepers, sit down on
one of the massive hand seats at the
back and give 'em a try. And if you've

Men only

Saks Fifth Avenue Men's Store

❶ 220 Post Street **☎** 415-986-
4300 **Ⓜ** Muni Metro F, J, K L, M, N;
bus 2, 3, 4, 9X, 30, 45; cable car
Powell-Mason, Powell-Hyde **🕑**
10am–7pm Mon–Wed and Sat;
10am–8pm Thu–Fri; noon–6pm Sun

Saks Fifth Avenue beats the
department store competition
(Macy's and Neiman Marcus)
by a nose, with five floors
dedicated to the hardened male
shopper. Men's ties, watches,
etc. hog the ground floor, with
the collections and designer-
wear interspersed throughout
the upper floors.

made a fashion mistake elsewhere, you can offload it here for ready money.
Can't be bad.

Mom's Body Shop

❶ 1408 Haight Street **☎** 415-864-6667 **Ⓜ** Muni Metro N; bus6, 7, 33, 37, 43
❶ noon–9pm daily

Somewhere between scary tattoo joint and sterile doctor's office, Mom's
Body Shop has a world-famous reputation for housing some of the West
Coast's best tattoo artists. Don't forget to bring your ID, there are strict age
restrictions. They'll also pierce anything you like as long as it'll heal. Perhaps
the place for that out-of-the-ordinary souvenir?

ANTIQUES AND HOMEWARES

ALABASTER

🛈 597 Hayes Street
📞 415-558-0482
www.alabastersf.com
🚇 Bus 16AX, 21, 22
🕐 11am–6pm Tues–Sat; noon–5pm Sun; closed Mon

Looking for something for your dream Pacific Heights apartment? Here you go. A very sexy store filled with predominantly white marble and Venetian-blown glass pieces to give your abode the stylish makeover it needs.

FUMIKI

🛈 2001 Union Street
📞 415-922-0573
🚇 Bus 41, 45
🕐 10am–6pm Mon–Sat; noon–5pm Sun

An expansive showroom featuring classic Japanese furniture, there's also a selection of smaller pieces, traditional chinaware and knick-knacks to make browsing an enjoyable experience.

LOFT

🛈 1823 Union Street
📞 415-674-0470
🚇 Bus 41, 45
🕐 10am–7pm Mon–Sat; 11am–7pm Sun

By turns a tacky little emporium and a stylish store, this fashionable interior and homewares store is situated smack bang in the centre of Cow Hollow and will tease you with everything from Paul Frank's monkey-logoed goodies to classy beech furniture.

Shop Around

Flex that plastic

ALL SHOPPED OUT

POMP

📍 516 Hayes Street
📞 415-864-1830
🕐 Noon–7pm daily

Small store with wallpaper-like home furnishings at an affordable price; from frames, cushions and general stuff to leather chairs and sideboards.

POTTERY BARN

📍 1 Embarcadero Center (Street Level), Sacramento Street
📞 415-788-6810
www.potterybarn.com
🚇 BART Embarcadero; Muni Metro F, J, K, L, M; bus 1, 41, 80X; cable car California
🕐 10am–7pm Mon–Fri

Depending on your taste, one of the US's biggest interiors chains offers furnishings that are either cute and comfy or bland and mainstream. Think *Little House on the Prairie* and you're not far off. The biggest store in San Francisco is in Stonestown.

WILLIAMS AND SONOMA

📍 2 Embarcadero Center
📞 415-421-2033
🚇 BART Embarcadero; Muni Metro F, J, K, L, M; bus 1, 41, 80X; cable car California

🕐 9.30am–7pm Mon–Sat; 11am–6pm Sun

Giving Crate and Barrel a run for its money in the cosy kitchen homewares department, Williams and Sonoma also offer a wide range of sauces, marinades, oils and the like.

BOOKS

THE BOOKSMITH

📍 1644 Haight Street
📞 415-863-8688
🚇 Muni Metro N; bus 7, 33, 37, 43
🕐 10am–6pm Mon–Sat; 10am–6pm Sun

A straightforward store and the best in the area, with a good selection of fiction and non-fiction.

BORDERS

📍 Union Square, corner of Powell and Post Streets
📞 415-399 1633
www.borders.com
🚇 BART Powell Street; Muni Metro F, J, K, L, M, N; bus 30, 38, 45,76 cable car Powell-Mason, Powell-Hyde
🕐 9am–11pm Mon–Wed; 9am–midnight Thu–Sat; 9am–9pm Sun

Tired of schlepping around those boutique bookstores? Couldn't give a monkey's about sniffing out the true literary San Francisco?

Well, let Borders bring it all to you the easy way.

A CLEAN WELL-LIGHTED PLACE FOR BOOKS

📍 Opera Plaza, 601 Van Ness Avenue
📞 415-441-6670
🚇 Metro F, K, L, M; bus 5, 16, 42, 47, 49
🕐 10am–11pm Mon–Sat; 11am–9pm Sun

Housed in an uninspiring grey concrete building near City Hall, A Clean Well-Lighted Place For Books might be clean, (relatively), well-lighted and well-loved, but it's not as inspiring as folk would have you believe. But with almost daily events and staff recommendations, it won't hurt to drop by if you're in the area.

A DIFFERENT LIGHT

📍 489 Castro Street
📞 415-431-0891
🚇 Muni Metro F, K, L, M; bus 24, 33, 35, 37
🕐 10am–midnight daily

You can trust the Castro to come up with the definitive gay/lesbian/transgender bookstore. And A Different Light doesn't disappoint, with its well-stocked selection of everything from non-fiction coffee-table tomes to comics. There are also in-store events and reading clubs for those bookworms who intend to stick around a little longer.

COSMETICS

SEPHORA
ⓘ 1 Stockton Street
ⓔ 415-392 1545
Ⓜ Muni Metro F, K, L, M, N; bus 9, 9X, 16AX, 30, 45
⊛ 10am–8pm Mon–Sat; 11am–7pm Sun

This downtown branch of the American brand store

offers an exquisite and extensive selection of top cosmetics, perfumes and skincare products. Perfumes are arranged alphabetically, and staff are very willing to talk you through any skincare issues. There's a branch at the airport.

FOOD

ANDREW ROTHSTEIN
ⓘ 2238 Polk Street
ⓔ 415-447 4094
andyfoods@aol.com
Ⓜ Bus 19, 30X, 42, 76
⊛ 11am–9pm Mon–Fri; 11am–8pm Sat–Sun

Upmarket deli and gourmet takeaway serving mouth-watering delights from Couscous Istanbul to simple Lemon Tarts.

GAY STUFF

DOES YOUR MOTHER KNOW?
ⓘ 4079 18th Street
Ⓜ Muni Metro F, K, L, M; bus 24, 33, 35, 37
⊛ 9.30am–10pm Mon–Thu; 9.30am–11pm Fri–Sat; 10am–9pm Sun

Compared to the other stores in the Castro, this offers a more sanitised

The definitive gay and lesbian bookstore

selection of gay flavoured merchandise, which your mother possibly could handle. Cards, wrapping paper, rainbow flag-wearing cuddly toys... you know the kind of thing. Does Your Father Know?, just down the road, offers a slightly edgier selection.

GOOD VIBRATIONS

ⓘ 1210 Valencia Street
ⓒ 415-974-8980
www.goodvibes.com
Ⓜ BART 24th Street; bus 14, 26, 48, 49, 67
☻ 11am–7pm Sun–Thu; 11am–8pm Fri–Sat

Probably the most famous sex shop in the world, Good Vibrations is an unforgettable experience. It's packed to the gills with every naughty toy imaginable, and the laid-back staff can advise you on every type of dildo and butt plug available in a size and colour to suit – they'll even help you locate your G-spot.

ROCK HARD

ⓘ 518 Castro Street
ⓒ 415-437-2430
Ⓜ Muni Metro F, K, L, M; bus 24, 33, 35, 37
☻ 9.30am–10pm Mon–Thu;

9.30am–midnight Fri–Sat; 10am–10pm Sun

Yep, here's where you can get the more hardcore stuff; sex toys, videos and DVDs, though Rock Hard also offer lines in cards, fridge magnets and some amusing 'erotic' statues.

LEATHER GOODS

COACH

ⓘ 190 Post Street
ⓒ 415-392-1772
Ⓜ BART Powell Station; bus 2, 3, 49, 9X, 30, 45; cable car Powell-Mason, Powell-Hyde
☻ 10am–7.30pm Mon–Sat; 11am–6pm Sun

Sexy, white-tiled store that will look after your leather goods needs. Frames, filofaxes, keyrings and even dogwear.

MENSWEAR

ABERCROMBIE AND FITCH

ⓘ 865 Market Street
ⓒ 415-284-9276
Ⓜ BART Powell Street; Muni Metro F, J, K, L, M; bus 9, 16AX, 26, 27, 31; cable car Powell-Mason, Powell-Hyde
☻ 9.30am–8pm Mon–Sat; 11am–6pm Sun

Washed-out looking and super-branded preppy wear that's becoming a worldwide fashion statement. Beautiful black-and-white marketing campaign featuring buff boys will help loosen your purse strings.

ARMANI EXCHANGE

ⓘ 2090 Union Street
ⓒ 415-749-0891
www.armaniexchange.com
Ⓜ Bus 22, 41, 45
☻ 10am–8pm Mon–Sat; 11am–6pm Sun

Branch of the designer diffusion range offering stylish shirts, sweaters and jeans at a more affordable price than its spendy namesake. It's worth checking out simply because you can't buy it in the UK. Womenswear too.

KENNETH COLE

ⓘ 166 Grant Avenue
ⓒ 415-981-2653
Ⓜ BART Powell Station; bus 9X, 9AX, 2, 3, 4, 30, 38, 45; cable car Powell-Mason, Powell-Hyde
☻ 10am–8pm Mon–Sat; noon–6pm Sun

The emphasis at Kenneth Cole is on leather goods, so definitely check out the range of sexy

Window display at Abercrombie and Fitch

shoes, but the affordable and sexy accessories are also superb. If you're with a lady friend, she'll lap up the sexiest womenswear. Kenneth Cole's sales rule.

LEVI'S STORE

- 🛈 300 Post Street
- 📠 415-501-0100
- Ⓜ BART Powell Station; bus 2, 3, 4, 9, 9AX, 38, 76; cable car Powell-Mason, Powell-Hyde
- 🕐 10am–8pm Mon–Sat; 11am–6pm Sun

If you're not shopping for your own jeans here, it's a sure thing that you'll be stocking up for someone else. And as San Francisco is the home of Levi's, it doesn't disappoint. Partly metal high-tech, partly wooden throwback, the store delivers denim, and its ever-growing fashion ranges over four fantastic floors.

MAC

- 🛈 5 Claude Lane
- 📠 415-837-0615
- Ⓜ BART Powell Station; bus 2, 3, 4, 9, 9AX, 38, 76; cable car Powell-Mason, Powell-Hyde
- 🕐 11am–6pm Mon–Sat; noon–6pm Sun

If you're looking for something a little different downtown. Neither high street nor high fashion, then MAC may have the answer. Edgier, off-the-wall menswear lines compete with retro-modern furnishings and artwork.

NIDA BOUTIQUE

- 🛈 2163 Union Street
- 📠 415-928-4670
- Ⓜ Bus 22, 41, 45
- 🕐 11am–7pm Mon–Sat; noon–6pm Sun

Tiny but well-stocked designer store featuring the labels Prada, Miu Miu and Helmut Lang.

ALL SHOPPED OUT

NIKETOWN

ℹ 278 Post Street
☎ 415-392-6453
Ⓜ BART Powell Station; bus 2, 3, 4, 9, 9AX, 38, 76; cable car Powell-Mason, Powell-Hyde
✪ 10am–8pm Mon–Sat; 11am–7pm Sun

Part shop, part marketing museum, Niketown might cover five floors or so, but ultimately there's only three levels of Nike goodies to check out, which are divided up by sport.

NOMADS

ℹ 556 Hayes Street
☎ 415-864-5697
Ⓜ Bus 16AX, 21, 22
✪ 11am–7pm Tues–Sat; 11am–6pm Sun–Mon

For discerning homies with a bit of cash to flash, here's the answer. DDCLab, Fred Perry and Blue Marlin feature, as well as edgier skatewear.

OLD NAVY

ℹ 801 Market at 4th Street **☎** 415-344-0375
www.oldnavy.com
Ⓜ BART Powell Station; bus 9X, 14X, 30, 45; cable car Powell-Mason, Powell-Hyde **✪** 9.30am–9pm Mon–Sat; 11am–8pm Sun

Like Banana Republic, the clothes on offer here are like the GAP's preppie range,

but this time the emphasis is on the cheap. And if you want to go really low, there's a discount area in the basement.

ROLO

ℹ 450 Castro Street
☎ 415–431-4545
info@rolo.com; shop online at www.kleptomaniac.com
Ⓜ Muni Metro F, K, L, M; bus 24, 33, 35, 37
✪ 11am–8pm Mon–Sat; 11am–7pm Sun

In the traditional gay schmutter-filled clothing stores of the Castro, this is the antidote if you're a homo homie. A no-frills white store – it looks like they've just moved in – it boasts the latest in B-boy fashion; oversized T-shirts, baggy pants, sneakers, etc. Labels include everything

from Stussy, Puma, Camper or Ben Sherman.

URBAN OUTFITTERS

ℹ 80 Powell Street
☎ 415-989-1515
Ⓜ BART Powell Street; Muni Metro F, J, K, L, M, N; bus 30, 38, 45,76; cable car Powell-Mason, Powell-Hyde **✪** 9.30am–9.30pm Mon– Sat; 10.30am–9pm Sun

Fast becoming an institution worldwide, this is still an essential stop-off for clothing, trainers and home-wares if you're a student – or just want to do it on the cheap with a touch of style.

MUSIC

VIRGIN RECORDS

ℹ 2 Stockton Street

Going casual on the Wharf

415-397-4525

BART Powell Street;
Muni Metro F, J, K, L, M, N;
bus 30, 38, 45,76; cable
car Powell-Mason, Powell-
Hyde

9.30am–9.30pm Mon–
Sat; 10.30am–9pm Sun

You'll know pretty
much what to expect,
but this is probably
the largest record
store in San Francisco
to indulge your main-
stream music, video,
book and magazine
requirements.

SECOND-HAND CLOTHES

COSTUMES ON HAIGHT

735 Haight Street

415-621-1356 email
cohceo@aol.com
www.citysearch.com/sfo/
costumeshaight

Muni Metro N; bus 6,
7, 22, 24, 61, 71

11am–7pm Mon–Sat;
noon–6pm Sun

If you're a diehard
thrift-store clothing
aficionado, then have
a poke around in
here. An intimidating
but all-encompassing
selection of second-
hand clothes which
spans the last half-
century is stuffed into
the smallest space.
They also offer a
fancy dress service.

SHOES

JOHN FLUEVOG SHOES

1697 Haight Street

415-436-9784

Muni Metro N; bus 6,
7, 33, 37, 43

11am–7pm Mon–Sat;
noon–6pm Sun

Haight really offers
the best shoe
selection in San Fran,
and John Fluevog's
range sits at the weird
end of it. While there
are a few wearable
options, this is for
someone who really
wants to stand out in
the crowd.

TOYS

SANRIO

39 Stockton Street

415-981-5568

BART Powell Station;
bus 9X, 14X, 27, 30, 31,
38, 45; cable car Powell-
Mason, Powell-Hyde

10am–8pm Mon–Sat;
11am–6pm Sun

You want kitsch?
Well, here's where
you start. Two
floors dedicated
to Hello Kitty and
other Sanrio 'toon
favourites: you can
pick up everything
from a frying pan to
an eraser – all
featuring Hello Kitty's
cute puss.

Jean Jeanie

San Francisco is the
original home of the
definitive denim
manufacturer, Levi's.

Jeans got their
big break during the
Gold Rush, which
kicked off in the city
from 1848, though
Levi Strauss actually
arrived five years
later. In the 1860s
he pioneered the
use of denim, and a
decade later he
added rivets to
strengthen the
material – miners
lapped up the new
type of workpants
and Levi Strauss'
company boomed.
Traditional 501s or
Engineered variety,
they are pretty
much an essential
fashion item and
have been a gay
staple since the
1970s.

If you're a Levi's
aficionado, there is
a museum at which
to pay homage (250
Valencia Street; tel
415-565-9159). To
visit you have to
book a tour, which
includes a video
and a visit to the
factory. If you just
wanna buy, head for
the megastore at
Union Square.

XYZ Restaurant at the W Hotel

Eating Out

Foodie heaven awaits you in San Francisco. If you can't eat well in this city, you'd be hard-pushed to find anywhere in the world to chow down, as the city brings global tastes and flavours to your table thanks to its diverse communities and its history as an international port of entry to the States.

With a fine culinary history dating back to the Gold Rush, the city capitalised on its reputation during the 1970s when it pioneered Californian cuisine, while the past decades have seen its number of ethnic restaurants increase. Throw in the fact that California is one of the most agriculturally rich parts of the States, and you can guarantee that the food will be fresh and of the highest quality – and it's none too expensive either, though there are lots of opportunities to splurge if you really want to.

Choice is rarely a problem, the number of restaurants in the city stretches into the thousands, with only Paris notching up a similar number. Just promise yourself you won't wind up in a total tourist trap – or worse still, fast-food hell.

Here's just a scratching of the surface...

Cream of the Cuisine

Ana Mandara

🛈 891 Beach Street. *Beach Street: see map p. 28* | 🚗 415-771-6800 | 🚌 Bus 19, 30, 42, 47, 49, 82X; cable car Powell-Hyde | 🕑 11.30am–2pm Mon–Fri; 5.30–9.30pm Sun–Thu; 5.30–10.30pm Fri–Sat | 🍴 🍴

> **The following price guides have been used for eating out and indicate the price for two courses:**
>
> 🍴 = cheap = under $10
>
> 🍴 = moderate = $10–$20
>
> 🍴 = expensive = over $20

Situated in prime tourist territory at Ghiradelli Square, you'd expect locals to keep well away, but it seems to be one of the San Franciscan foodie haunts. Like a soundstage inside, Ana Mandara is filled with colonial glamour and ethnic relics, but offers upmarket and delicious Vietnamese cooking with that all-important contemporary twist. Salivate at the promise of crispy lobster ravioli and wokked tournedos of beef tenderloin with sweet onion and peppercress – and definitely try the Ana Mandara cocktail. Sublime. So it's a bit pricey and the clientele a bit dressy, but it's worth it all for a first-class eating experience.

Aqua

Try something fishy

ℹ️ 252 California Street. *See map p. 34*
📞 415-956-9662 🚇 BART Embarcadero; Muni Metro F, J, K, L, M, N; bus 1, 15, 31, 38AX, 42, 80X; cable car: California
🕐 11.30am–2.30pm Mon–Fri; 5.30–10.30pm Mon–Thu and Sun; 5.30–11pm Fri–Sat

Situated in the Financial District just around the corner from the Mandarin Oriental, so you know you're in for a treat. And Aqua delivers. The interior might be a tad 1980s, with beige furnishings and oversized flower displays, but for seafood you can't fault this place. Relish the prospect of crispy skin black bass, pancetta-wrapped Atlantic salmon or roasted Alaskan halibut, although there is a vegetarian option available. With attentive staff and nice touches like complimentary soup taster and post-dinner chocolates, this is a luxurious eating experience. No wonder booking is near-on essential.

Betelnut

ℹ️ 2030 Union Street. *Union Street: see map p. 62* 📞 415-929-8855 🚇 Bus 22, 41, 45 🕐 11.30am–11pm Mon–Thu and Sun; 11am–midnight Fri–Sat

Another Asian masterpiece, this time offering modern-day dishes from across China, Korea, Japan, Thailand and Vietnam. Situated at the heart of Union Street in Cow Hollow, it's worth nabbing a pavement table to check out the shoppers, but this place also comes into its own in the evening. Essentially, it's a stylish theme restaurant with red lacquer tables, dark wood furnishings and tasteful Art-Deco Chinese beer ads, but it serves up tasty meals from chilli-crusted calamari through Asian salads to oven-smoked sea bass.

Zuni Café

ℹ️ 1658 Market Street 📞 514-552-2522
🚇 BART Van Ness; Muni Metro F, J, K, L, M, N; bus 6, 7, 42, 47, 49, 66, 71
🕐 11.30am–3pm daily; 3–6pm Tues–Sat; 6pm–midnight Tues–Sun

While there's nothing unique about the range of Californian food at Zuni Café, it's a pretty special place and an ideal setting for a weekend brunch. Sitting out of place on Market Street among a straggle of antique/junk stores, Zuni Café is a glass-panelled bistro that's light, airy and filled with a funky urban crowd of twentysomethings revelling in the chilled-out atmosphere. An enviably stocked copper bar runs along the café side, and if you want the slightly more upscale restaurant dining experience, just head on into the room out back, though you should feel right on home wherever you are. And do sup on one of their superior Bloody Marys and wonder how they make them so good. Very San Francisco.

At the Cypress Club

XYZ

 181 3rd Street at Howard Street. *3rd Street: see map p. 46* 415-817-7836

Bus 12, 14X, 15, 30, 45, 76

8–11am and 11.30am–2.30pm Mon–Fri; 8am–2.30pm Sat–Sun; 5.30–10pm daily

Unlike New York City, San Francisco is not known for its Prada-clad, all-in-black ladies and gentlemen. But if that's your bag, then get yourself to the very swish W Hotel's restaurant, XYZ – get it?

Normally hotel restaurants are a little ropey around the edges, but XYZ has got it all right. In spades. Serving up some of the cleverest and most fabulous grub in the city, its menu is contemporary, with a Pan Asian/Pacific Rim thing going on.

The wine menu is well-informed, and all the best Californian ingredients are used in the meals, so indulge your love of quality delicacies and you won't be disappointed.

Cool surroundings, funky clientele and sexily-clad waiters abound. Dress up a little and you'll feel right at home.

Wasabi and Ginger

 2299 Van Ness at Vallejo Street. *Van Ness and Vallejo Street: map p. 40*

415-345-1368

www.wasabiandginger.com

Bus 30X, 42, 47, 49

5pm–10.30pm daily

Wasabi and Ginger is one of many good-quality and budget-pleasing *sushi* bars in San Francisco. Presided over by a live audience in the aquarium, the décor might be un-original, but it's clean, cheap and the *sushi* is fantastic – no wonder the locals seem to cherish it. The take-away trade is also big business. Big old slabs of *sushi* will please, but a standing ovation goes to the Wasabi and Ginger Martini (tuna, salmon, avocado and *tobiko*, lightly fried and served in a cocktail glass). Be sure to check out the Robata, the skewer and barbecued selection, too.

Dottie's True Blue Cafe

 522 Jones Street, between Geary and O'Farrell Streets. *Jones Street: see map p. 20*

415-885-2767

Bus 2, 3, 4, 27, 38

7.30am–2pm Mon and Wed–Sun

You can't come to the States and not do the all-American breakfast thing, and Dottie's provides the quintessential experience. Not much more than one room, it's decorated with big blue cup murals, black-and-white photos of Josephine Baker and Dorothy Dandridge – and you can even eat your breakfast off Greta Garbo's face.

All this while charming staff deliver hefty but yummy portions of French toast, pancakes, eggs, etc. to anyone and everyone.

Super-busy at the weekends, be warned: you'll probably have to queue.

Dining at Dottie's

Eating alfresco

Luna Park

694 Valencia Street at 18th Street. *Valencia Street: see map p. 52*

415-553-8585 www.lunaparksf.com

BART: 16th Street; bus 14, 26, 33, 49

1.30–2.30pm Mon–Fri; 5.30–10.30pm Mon–Thu; 5.30–11pm Fri–Sat; 5.30–10pm Sun

At the time of writing, all of San Francisco was a-buzz with Luna Park. The latest arrival in the increasingly trendy Mission District, it turns its back on over-fashioned cuisine, delivering instead top-quality, straightforward, good ol' American cooking, but with a few twists. Think pork chops, flat-iron steak, lamb shank, king salmon. It looks like an upmarket but smallish Mexican restaurant with secluded booths, red walls and screwy art, and is frequented mostly by yuppies who seem to be taking the area to their heart. You'll probably have to book if the trend continues, though you might be able to squeeze in at the bar.

A taste of Mexico

Café Flore

ℹ️ 2298 Market Street. *See map p. 70*
📞 415-621-8579 Ⓜ Muni Metro F, K, L,
M; bus 24, 35, 37 ☯️ 7am–11.30pm
Mon–Thu and Sun; 7.30am– midnight
Fri–Sat 🍴 🎫

OK, so it's a little bit shabby around
the edges, but you get the impression Café Flore is as loved by its
punters as Judy Garland. There
might not always be gold at the
end of the rainbow here, but it does
benefit from a prime location in
the Castro. The locals flock here to
do their homework, read books,
hang with their neighbours, cruise
and eat the kind of food Mom
used to make. There's a fantastic
selection of bread and pastries as
well as home-cooked food. Order
at the bar round the corner.

La Rondalla

ℹ️ 901 Valencia Street at 20th Street.
Valencia Street: see map p. 52
📞 415-647-7474 Ⓜ Bus 14, 26, 49
☯️ 11.30am–3.30am Tues–Sun 🍴 🎫

If you're after Mexican food in the
Mission, there's a couple of *taquerias*
worth checking. The dark little
Puerto Allegre (546 Vallencia Street;
tel 415-255-8201) is a winner and
always packed, but down the road
La Rondalla offers a more authentic
experience, even if the food isn't
brilliant. Essentially, it's a straightforward little diner with red booths
and stuffed animal heads gaze over a
mixed local crowd, assisted by
Mexican mamas and *mariachis*. Take
your pick from *tacos, enchiladas, fajitas*
and combination specials. And don't
forget the margaritas.

EATING OUT

Best of the Rest

UNION SQUARE, CHINATOWN AND NORTH BEACH

BLACK CAT
 501 Broadway at Kearny
415-981-2233
Bus 12, 15, 30, 41, 83
5.30–11.15pm Mon–Thu; 5.30pm– 12.15am Fri–Sat

A self-proclaimed '*Bistro des poetes*', Black Cat is an institution in North Beach and offers a rolling daily menu of French food – with an emphasis on seafood – in tasteful, if typical American brasserie surroundings . The real deal here, though, is the live music with dancing and hi-jinx in the basement.

BRANDY HO'S
217 Columbus Avenue
415-788-7527
Bus 9AX, 12, 15, 30, 41, 83
11.30am–11pm Mon–Thu and Sun; 11.30am–midnight Fri–Sat

If you're determined to sample Chinese food in Chinatown, why not try *San Francisco Guardian* readers' number one choice? Brandy Ho's won't offer you much in décor, but it will touch base with its tasty, spicy dishes from the Hunan province.

CAFE DE LA PRESSE
352 Grant Avenue
415-392-3505
BART Montgomery Street; Muni Metro F, J, K, L, M, N; bus 2, 3, 4, 15, 30, 45, 76 7am–11pm daily

The '*la presse*' of its name refers to its well-stocked shelves of glossies and international newspapers, but essentially this is an Americanised French café for a coolish crowd of all ages. It offers a menu which sees *croque monsieur* nestling next to American classics. Try the calorie-fest that is their onion soup.

CAFFE TRIESTE
601 Vallejo Street
415-392-6739
Bus 12, 15, 41, 83
6.30am–11pm Mon–Thu and Sun; 6.30am–midnight Fri–Sat

Anyone would feel at home in Caffè Trieste, with its cosy ochre mural-covered walls, though there is a tendency for the arty Beatnik crowd to hang out here and partake of the smooth coffees/ read the paper/write copious notes/do whatever wannabe Beatniks do.

ENRICO'S

 504 Broadway
415-982-6223
Bus 12, 15, 30, 41, 83
11.30am–5pm Mon–Sat; 11.30am–4pm Sun

The name has real resonance in the North Beach area, and it's a fancy Art-Deco-styled restaurant offering quality Italian food and jazz on a nightly basis. Food is mainly a straight-forward, modern Italian mix with great pasta. All first-rate.

FIOR D'ITALIA

601 Union Street
415-986-1886
Bus 15, 30, 39, 41, 45
11.30am–10.30pm daily

Established in 1886, it's one of the oldest restaurants in San Francisco and looks like any Italian

restaurant, with a mural, long wooden bar and even 'comedy' blackboard menu and tables outside. The food is good, if heavy, and its Old World range is extensive, covering everything from pasta, meat, fish and rice right through to a classic polenta.

GELATO CLASSICO CLUB

576 Union Street
415-391-6667
Bus 15, 30, 39, 41, 45
Noon–10pm Mon–Thu and Sun; noon–11pm Fri–Sat

A handy though tiny gelateria tucked away in North Beach. Do give it a whirl, however, as all the ice-creams are homemade. There are

a couple of tables, but you might want to relax with your cone in Washington Square round the corner.

THE HOUSE

 1230 Grant Avenue
415-986-8612
Bus 12, 15, 30, 41
11.30am–3pm Mon–Fri; 5.30–10pm Mon–Thu; 5.30–11pm Fri; 5–11pm Sun

It might have the stylish look of one of its Italian neighbours, with its slate tiles, blank walls and white tablecloths, but The House's heart is Asian. After a tasty appetiser of cucumber and sesame seeds, it offers fusion snack dishes and salads, as well as mains like Korean red pepper-flecked lamb.

French or Italian tonight?

EATING OUT

MOCCA

ⓘ 175 Maiden Lane

✆ 415-956-1188

Ⓜ BART Powell; Muni
Metro F, J, K, L, M, N ;
bus 2, 3, 4, 30, 35, 45
cable car Powell-Hyde,
Powell-Mason

✹ 9.30am–4.30pm daily

🍴 **🍷**

If you've been
shopping hard in
Union Square, you'll
be in need of swish-
looking Mocca,
which offers luxury
sandwiches and
mouth-watering
salads, all with an
Italian flavour. There
are tables and chairs
on the paved-over
street outside.

MOOSE'S

ⓘ 1652 Stockton Street

✆ 415-989-7800

Ⓜ Bus 15, 30, 39, 41, 45

✹ 11.30am–2.30pm
Thu–Sat; 10am–2.30pm
Sun; 5.30–10.30pm Sun–
Thu; 5.30–11.30pm Sat

🍴 **🍷**

Moose's is a typical
but simple old-school
American brasserie on
Washington Square.
While it won't attract
the cool crowd, it
continues to please a
fortysomething
clientele who go for
its wonderful Califor-
nian cuisine. This
ranges from Maine
crab and leek tart to
spinach and ricotta

tortelli. Tasty brunch
menu on Sunday too.

L'OSTERIA DEL FORNO

ⓘ 519 Columbus
Avenue

✆ 415-982-1124

Ⓜ Bus 15, 30, 31, 40

✹ 11.30am–10pm
Sun–Mon and Wed–Thu;
11.30am–10.30pm Fri–Sat

🍴 **🍷**

A simple, tiny but
authentic-looking
Italian restaurant
which offers
traditional Italian
fare, though you
should try one of
their thin'n'crispy
pizzas, cooked in a
brick-lined oven.
Pastas are usually
specials, but fantastic.

SEARS' FINE FOODS

ⓘ 439 Powell Street

✆ 415-986-1160

Ⓜ BART Powell; Muni
Metro F, J, K, L, M, N; bus
2, 3, 4, 30, 35; cable car
Powell-Mason, Powell-
Hyde

✹ 6.30am–2.30pm daily

🍴 **🍷**

If you're staying near
Union Square, this
could be a handy
little joint for you.
Part diner, part
restaurant, it comes
complete with
counter seating,
shocking pink walls
and revolving desserts

in a glass case. Check
out the hefty if
straightforward all-
American breakfasts.

YOU'S DIM SUM

ⓘ 675 Broadway

✆ 415-788-7028

Ⓜ Bus 12, 15, 30, 41

✹ 7am–7pm daily

🍴 **🍷**

On the edge of
Chinatown, this place
specialises in *dim sum*.
Point to your choice
of dumplings from
one of the vats at the
front of house, then
retire to the pink
plastic tables at the
back to relish. There
are also a few rice
dishes and steamed
greens.

TELEGRAPH HILL, THE EMBARCADERO AND FINANCIAL DISTRICT

CYPRESS CLUB

ⓘ 500 Jackson Street

✆ 415-296-8555

Ⓜ Bus 12, 15, 30X, 41,
83

✹ 5.30pm–10pm
Sun–Thu; 5.30pm–11pm
Fri–Sat

🍴 **🍷**

Feel the urge to
splurge? Cypress
Club will deliver
first-rate, innovative
food at a price, but
hey, it is in the

All American

interior alone. It's comfy but kinda stylish. As for the food, traditional but yummy fare at a decent price.

POLKERS GOURMET BURGERS

- 2226 Polk Street
- 415-885-1000
- Bus 19, 27, 83
- 11am–11pm daily

With its dark wood booths and cream walls, this twist on a diner theme looks more promising from the outside than it actually is. Nevertheless, its focus is any kind of burger served whichever way you want, from basic to barbecue to teriyaki. Sandwiches too.

TITANIC CAFE

- Commodore Hotel, 825 Sutter Street
- 415-928-8870
- Bus 2, 3, 4
- 7am–2pm daily

A simple, tiny diner annexed to the Commodore Hotel. Breakfasts are its strong point, delivering quality but straightforward fare with a *Titanic* twist.

Financial District. Just check out the voluptuous Dali-esque interior and enjoy the top-notch service.

WATERFRONT CAFE

- Pier 7, Embarcadero
- 415-391-2696
- Muni Metro F
- 11am–4pm and 5.30–10.30pm Mon–Sat; 10am–4.30pm Sun

If you want to eat by the water, then the traditional Waterfront Café is the perfect spot, though if you want to relax inside, the surroundings are traditional and grand. Innovative seafood is what to try – like San Francisco's famous clam chowder – though there's steak and a couple of vegetarian dishes.

RUSSIAN HILL, NOB HILL AND TENDERLOIN

CAFE BEAN

- 754 Post Street
- 415-776-6620
- Bus 2, 3, 4, 27, 76
- 6am–7pm daily

This is a delightful little café offering breakfasts, sandwiches, quick-fix goodies and superior coffee.

LEMONGRASS

- 2348 Polk Street
- 415-929-1183
- Bus 19, 30, 41, 45, 76
- 11am–10pm daily

A big up goes to Lemongrass for its

EATING OUT

SOMA

CLOUDS RESTAURANT
🛈 Yerba Buena Gardens, 720 Howard Street
📞 415-278-0432
🚌 Bus 15, 30, 45, 76
🍴 🍽️

A glass-fronted, airy restaurant with outdoor seating. The food won't surprise. as it's typical but good American fare like Caesar salads, burgers, tuna and pastas.

THE MISSION

BLOWFISH SUSHI
🛈 2170 Bryant Street
🚌 Bus 27
🕐 11.30am–10.30pm Mon–Thu and Sun; 11.30am–11.30pm Fri–Sat
🍴 🍽️

A bit off the beaten track, but Blowfish Sushi has fast become legendary. as an upscale, trendy bar.

FOREIGN CINEMA
🛈 2534 Mission Street
📞 415-648-7600
🚌 BART 24th Street; bus 14, 49
🕐 6–10.30pm Tues–Sun
🍴 🍽️

Yes, it is pretentious watching art-house movies while you eat dinner, so it probably

makes sense that the food is French. Meaty mains, although the vegetarian option is sublime. Ask for the patio if you want to catch the movie.

SLANTED DOOR
🛈 584 Valencia Street
📞 415-861-8032
🚌 BART 16th Street; bus 22, 26, 53
🕐 11.30am–3pm and 5.30–10pm Tues–Sun
🍴 🍽️

Slanted Door was a favourite long before the Mission's culinary breakthrough, and it continues to kick culinary ass. Rustic Vietnamese food at lunchtime, and more delicate at night. Booking is essential.

JAPANTOWN, PACIFIC HEIGHTS AND COW HOLLOW

GREENS
🛈 Fort Mason Center, Marina Boulevard
📞 415-771-6222
🚌 Bus 22, 28
🕐 5.30–9.30pm Mon; 11.30am–2pm Tues–Fri; 11.30am–2.30pm Sat; 10am–2pm Sun
🍴 🍽️

A converted barracks is the unlikely setting for this vegetarian restaurant. Even if

it weren't for the jaw-dropping views, the top tucker would make it worthwhile, as it delivers a sumptuous selection using ingredients from its own Green Gulch Farm.

HAIGHT ASHBURY AND THE CASTRO

BAGHDAD CAFE
🛈 2295 Market Street
📞 415-621-4434
🚌 Muni Metro F, J, K, L, M; bus 24, 33, 35, 37
🕐 24 hours daily
🍴 🍽️

Best for a post-club binge or a Sunday morning brunch with its selection of diner fare. Nice staff, and a Castro crowd.

CAFE CUVEE
🛈 2073 Market Street
📞 415-621 7488
🕐 6pm–midnight Mon–Thu; 6pm–2am Fri–Sat
🚌 BART Church Street Station; Muni Metro F, J, K, L, M; bus 22, 37
🍴 🍽️

While it looks straightforward, if not a bit 90s, the emphasis is on the food, which comes acclaimed.

RESTAURANT FINDER

American

Baghdad Café	102
Café Cuvée	102
Clouds Restaurant	102
Cypress Club	100
Luna Park	96
Moose's	100
Polkers Gourmet Burgers	101
Red Grill	103
Sears' Fine Foods	100
Titanic Café	101
2223 Market	103
XYZ	95
Zuni Café	94

Asian

Betelnut	94
The House	99

Cafés

Café Bean	101
Café de la Presse	98
Café Flore	97
Caffé Trieste	98
Dottie's True Blue Café	96
Gelato Classico Club	99
Mocca	100

Chinese

Brandy Ho's	98
You's Dim Sum	100

French

Black Cat	98
Foreign Cinema	102

Italian

Enrico's	99
Fior d'Italia	99
L'Osteria del Forno	100

Japanese

Blowfish Sushi	102
Wasabi and Ginger	95

Mexican

La Rondalla	97

Seafood

Aqua	94
Waterfront Café	101

Thai

Lemongrass	101

Vegetarian

Greens	102

Vietnamese

Ana Mandara	93
Slanted Door	102

RED GRILL

- 4063 18th Street
- 415-255-2733
- Bus 24, 35, 37
- 5pm–midnight daily

Pulling an upwardly mobile gay clientele mostly in their thirties, who come for steaks and fresh seafood.

2223 MARKET

- 2223 Market Street
- 415-431-0692
- Muni Metro F, K, L, M; bus 24, 37
- 6.30–10pm Mon–Thu and Sun; 6.30–11pm Fri–Sat; 10am–2pm Sun

A popular restaurant (booking advised). It's a white tablecloths, muted lighting kind of place. Modern American cooking with Italian influences.

The Red Room

Cool and Cosmopolitan

Out on the Town

It will come as no surprise that the majority of San Francisco's gay nightlife takes place in and around the Castro and the Mission, hence the emphasis in this guide. However, there is some action to be had in places like Polk Street, as well as a handful of nice straight bars to which we should give the benefit of the doubt.

Below is just a selection, and bear in mind that like anywhere else in the world, things go in and out of favour, so it's worth double-checking in the local listings mags once you arrive. The *Bay Area Reporter* will fill you in on the latest news for the community, the *San Francisco Frontiers News Magazine* goes one better with all-encompassing listings, *Odyssey* gives you the low-down from the club scene and the CD-sized *Free* magazine will deliver an extensive night-by-night guide across the board. You can pick these mags up in the majority of the gay bars below.

My Top Clubs

Badlands

4121 18th Street | 415-626-9320 | Muni Metro F, K, L, M; bus 35, 37
2pm–2am daily

Badlands is a recent addition to the Castro scene and takes the concept of the video bar up a notch. A semi-high-tech steel and raw-bricked environment is the setting for video screens blasting the latest gay-friendly videos to a young, strutty crowd.

There's even a dance area out back for you to really let it go – while up front it's a tad more friendly and cruisey. Lots of gentlemen, lots of posing, but lots of fun too.

The Café

ⓘ 2367 Market Street | **☎** 415-861-3846 | **Ⓜ** Muni Metro F, K, L, M; bus 35, 37 | **✸**
1pm–2am daily

Formerly the Café San Marcos, The Café can be relied on to deliver the
goods – particularly at the weekend, when you'll probably have to queue
up outside. It's hot'n'sweaty'n'dark with a small dancefloor, two bars and
a patio. But its young, fun-loving and not over-trendy boy'n'
girl crowd seem to love it and the latest dance anthems it plays.
Apparently, it's Ellen DeGeneres' favourite hangout in the city, and let's
face it, she's right: you can't go
wrong here for a good night out.

Pleasuredome

ⓘ 177 Townsend Street | **☎** 415-289-
6699 | **Ⓜ** Bus 30, 42, 45, 76
✸ 9pm–7am Fri–Sat; 9pm– 3.30am Sun

Currently the best place to ogle
buffed-up twentysomething
muscle boys. Take off your T-shirt
and get on down to the hardest of
beats. Pleasuredome is San
Francisco's biggest gay club, which
is re-branded Club Universe on a
Saturday. It's a large, darkened
warehouse with two bars – one of
which will even serve you with
power drinks – and a low-key
chill-out room, all sparsely
furnished in industrial style.

Martuni's

ⓘ 4 Valencia Street | **☎** 415-241-0205
Ⓜ Muni Metro F, J, K, L, M; bus 26
✸ 4pm–2am daily

If you've always wanted to sit at the
bar sipping a freshly-shaken Martini
while a pianist tinkles lightly in the
background, then don't miss
Martuni's. It's a dark and intimate

Esta Noche

ⓘ 3079 16th Street | **☎** 415-861-
5757 | **Ⓜ** BART 16th Street; bus 14,
22, 26, 49, 53 | **✸** 2pm–2am daily

OK, so it's a scrubby, tiny bar
that isn't much to look at either
from outside or inside, but
where else are you going to
check out lip-synching drag
queens or muscle boy strippers,
all of a Latin nature? It's
frequented by a mixed Hispanic/
white crowd in their 20s and 30s
who really let their hair down.
It's also fairly busy nightly at
showtime, usually around 11pm.

Let your hair down

little place with two rooms and a kind of patio entrance. It obviously draws
in an older, 30-plus crowd, though anyone would feel right at home with
its flavoured Martinis (watermelon, raspberry, etc.), a Peach Fuzz or a
Razzle Dazzle at $7 a go.

The Red Room

🛈 827 Sutter Street
📞 415-346-7666
Ⓜ Bus 2, 3,4, 27
🕐 5pm–2am daily

The Red Room is indeed that. Admittedly not the biggest space in town, this is still a stylishly done-out place. There's even a wall made of bottles, while the staff whisk up top Cosmopolitans for a crowd of hipsters who occasionally spill out onto the street. As cool as it is, its success is all about location: where else are you going to enjoy a real cool cocktail experience downtown?

Mecca

🛈 2029 Market Street
📞 415-621-7000
Ⓜ Muni Metro F, J, K, L, M, N; bus 22
🕐 5pm–1.30am daily

Trendy and upwardly mobile straight folk and gay guys come here for the huge oval bar in the centre, which has a selection of *grappa* encircling the middle pillar. It's a massive dark space with booths, white tablecloths and metallic furniture – like an upmarket hotel bar. Very nice.

The Midnight Sun

🛈 4067 18th Street 📞 415-861-4186 Ⓜ Muni Metro F, K, L, M; bus 33, 35 🕐 Noon–2am daily

A tile-fronted bar with an inset video screen on the outside, this cruisey drinking establishment always seems to be busy and is a perfect place to hang out. It's quite small, but not really intimidating, with a 20s to 30s largely male crowd. With a lengthy, well-stocked bar, it's seemingly become an institution, with giant video screens interspersing the current dance hits with clips of *Mommie Dearest, Golden Girls, Dynasty* and other camp classics. Much fun.

Beauty Bar

🛈 2299 Mission Street
📞 415-552-7788
Ⓜ Bus 14, 49
🕐 5pm–2am Mon–Fri; 7pm–2am Sat–Sun

Yep, it's hair salon-meets-bar in this funky Mission hangout. It's modelled on the New York drinking establishment of the same name, so check out the grungy 50s retro furnishings: chandeliers, dressing table and yes, you can even sit under hairdryers if you're having a bad hair day! The concept might all sound rather 'hair now, gone tomorrow', but it's still pulling in the trendy-ish, straight punters. A cute pit stop en route home.

Lexington Club

🛈 3464 19th Street
📞 415-863-2052
Ⓜ Bus 14, 26, 33, 49
🕐 3pm–2am daily

Despite the city's huge lesbian population, currently San Francisco only offers one permanent dyke bar. A mashed-up mix of cute skaters, indie kids and generic Californian dykes kick back to grunge rock and classic tunes in this large bar. Cheap drinks, friendly staff and an ever-busy pool table offset the slightly dingy settings.

All Clubbed Out

THE CASTRO

THE BAR ON CASTRO

| ❶ 456 Castro Street,
| ✆ 415-626-1061
| Ⓜ Muni Metro F; bus 33, 35, 37
| 🕐 3pm–2am Mon–Fri; noon–2am Sat–Sun

A groovy little find where a less-typical crowd seems to hang out. Loungey and dark, with a live DJ at the weekend playing a housey selection.

BLOW BUDDIES

| ❶ 933 Harrison Street
| ✆ 415-863-4323
www.blowbuddies.com
| Ⓜ Bus 27, 42
| 🕐 7.30pm–3am Thu; 9pm–4am Fri–Sat; 6pm–midnight Wed; varying according to event
| 🎟 Membership $3; entry $8

A private club with strict dress policy running Thu–Sun. It's best to phone first or check out their website for all the ins and outs.

DETOUR

| ❶ 2348 Market Street
| ✆ 415-861-6053
| Ⓜ Muni Metro F; bus 37
| 🕐 2pm–2am daily

A dark sleazy bar – definitely cruising-compatible. The crowd is generally under 30. A chain-link fence runs right down the middle of the bar, with high-rise benches either side, so you can relax and maintain eye contact at the same time. How thoughtful is that? There are also pinball machines, bumping music and beefy go-gos.

HARVEYS

| ❶ 500 Castro Street
| ✆ 415-431-4278
| Ⓜ Bus 24, 33, 35
| 🕐 11am–midnight Mon–Thu; 9am–2am Fri–Sun

There are two branches of this Hard Rock Café-like venue, with the more stylish one on less desirable Polk Street. Named after out-gay politician Harvey Milk, there's a selection of his and other gay icons' memorabilia on the walls. Friendly staff and a typical Castro clientele.

METRO

| ❶ 3600 16th Street
| ✆ 415-703-9750
| Ⓜ Muni Metro K, L, M; bus 37
| 🕐 4.30pm–2am Mon–Fri; 1pm–2am Sat–Sun

Metro is a generic, but quite nice mixed/gay bar. Low-key, but featuring typical video screens and gay music, it's got a dark interior, cute bar staff and a Chinese restaurant .

SOMA

THE STUD
🛈 399 Ninth Street
📞 415-863-6623
🚌 Bus 19, 27, 42
🕐 5pm–2am daily

Thirty-five years old, the Stud is a dark, down-to-earth bar-cum-nightclub, which can attract literally anybody with a gay bone in their body. It's also buried in the wastelands of SOMA, so be sure you want to go there before forking out for a taxi. Give 'em a call first.
 The End-Up (401 Sixth Street; tel 415-357-0827) is a few blocks away, so you could kill two birds with one stone. Its Sunday Tea Dances, kicking off at 6am, are legendary.

THE MISSION

LASZLO'S
🛈 2532 Mission Street
🚌 BART 24th Street; bus 14, 33, 39
🕐 6pm–2am daily

Attached to the über-trendy Foreign Cinema, Lazslo's has a

grey interior, low-key lighting and views across the Mission. One to watch.

RUSSIAN HILL

THE CINCH SALOON
🛈 1723 Polk Street
📞 415-776-4162
🚌 Bus 19, 27, 42, 49
🕐 6am–2am daily

'John Wayne on the outside, Carmen Miranda inside'. This local bar seems to appeal to older gay folk. Saloon-bar doors and 17 draft beers.

TONIC
🛈 2360 Polk Street
📞 415-771-5535
🚌 Bus 19, 41, 45
🕐 4pm–2am daily

Tonic is a local but groovy bar, which

attracts a straight but trendy crowd in their late 20s. It's a sexy little place that's worth popping your head around the door.

NOB HILL

NOB HILL ADULT THEATER
🛈 729 Bush Street
📞 415-976-2244
🚌 Bus 1, 31, 38; cable car Powell-Mason
🕐 8pm–2.30am Sun–Wed; 8pm–3am Thu–Sat

'Famous from the day we opened' boasts the Theater, and indeed it's got some reputation. Cough up $30 (or $20 before noon) and enter hunk heaven with half-hourly live strip shows, where you can tip the fella for an extra wiggle.

Hunk heaven

Book your seats for the Castro Theatre

Playing Around Town

If you're looking for an alternative culture on the West Coast, San Francisco is really where it's at. What Los Angeles offers in terms of blockbuster movies, San Francisco can rival with the highbrow and the arthouse – though if you want candy-floss for the brain, that shouldn't be a problem either.

San Franciscans love going to the movies. As well as some major state-of-the-art cineplexes, there's also an impressive alternative film scene, as well as the world's biggest lesbian and gay film festival. It's also home to directors like Francis Ford Coppola and George Lucas.

There aren't many of San Francisco's beautiful old movie theatres left. Like most cities, it's been prey to the multiplexes. Sony's Metreon is one of the best, with 15 screens in a high-tech complex-cum-mall. It is something of an experience – with big old comfy seats and amazing sound.

San Franciscans' appetite for art-house and foreign cinema is reflected in its independent movie houses, many of which are run by a chain called Landmark (415-352-0810).

The theatre and dance scene does have some good venues and local performers. With Broadway-style extrava-ganzas, fringe theatre, opera and experimental dance, there's something for everyone. Get tickets through BASS, the ticket brokers (415-776-1999). They have outlets all over the city, but you pay for this with a whopping surcharge. For cut-price, same-day tickets for theatre productions, dance and opera, try TIX Bay Area in Union Square (cash only, but they take advance credit card bookings). As well as the pack 'em in theatres and performance spaces, San Francisco has several smaller, funkier venues. Again, check local press for info.

PLAYING AROUND TOWN

Whatever your bag, there are plenty of live music venues, and throughout the years the city's been home to many icons, like Billie Holiday, Janis Joplin, Jefferson Airplane, the Dead Kennedys and the Grateful Dead.

The Great American Music Hall attracts all manner of artists from A-list to local, r'n'b to folk, and has a pretty impressive interior. But if your tastes are a bit more 'out there', check out Justice League, one of the city's most popular venues, which draws in everything from live acts to DJs. If you dig jazz, Fillmore Auditorium is your best bet, while the Boom Boom Room should do you for blues. Get your tickets direct from the box office to avoid paying inflated booking fees.

OUTLINES

CASTRO THEATER

- **ⓘ** 429 Castro Street
- **ⓒ** 415-621 6120
- **Ⓜ** Muni Metro F, J, K, L, M; bus 24, 35, 37;

As well as being a Castro symbol, this theatre also offers a full-on old-style cinematic experience – there's even a little organ player doing his business in the interludes. Check local press for what's on – anything from black-and-white classics to new gay cinema to director's cuts.

CURRAN THEATER

- **ⓘ** 445 Geary Street
- **ⓒ** 415-551-2000
- www.bestofbroadway-sf.com
- **Ⓜ** BART Powell Street; Muni Metro F, J, K, L, M, N; bus 2, 3, 4, 27, 38

Mainstream Broadway-style productions.

EUREKA THEATER COMPANY

- **ⓘ** 215 Jackson Street
- **ⓒ** 415-788-7469
- www.eurekatheater.org
- **Ⓜ** Bus 12, 42, 83

Edgy new stuff.

INTERSECTION FOR THE ARTS

- **ⓘ** 446 Valencia Street
- **ⓒ** 415-626-2787
- **Ⓜ** BART 16th Street; bus 14, 22, 26, 49, 53
- **Ⓝ** No credit cards

One of San Francisco's favourite cutting-edge arts centres, with a theatre and exhibition spaces.

THE RED VIC

- **ⓘ** 1727 Haight Street
- **ⓒ** 415-668-3994
- **Ⓜ** Bus 6, 7, 66, 71

Also home to a bijou art gallery and even cuter B&B (see page 132), chill out on bashed-up leather sofas, munch on popcorn and enjoy alternative cinema.

THE ROXIE

- **ⓘ** 3117 16th Street
- **ⓒ** 415-863-1087
- **Ⓜ** BART 16th Street; bus 22, 26, 53

Expect an eclectic array of movies, including everything from art house to trashy horrors. It's the not the comfiest of cinemas, but you're not there for plushness, you're there for the vibe, man.

SAN FRANCISCO BALLET

- **ⓘ** War Memorial Opera House, 301 Van Ness Avenue
- **ⓒ** 415-865-2000

www.sfballet.org

🚇 BART Civic Center;
Muni Metro F, J, K, L, M, N;
bus 21, 42, 47, 49

America's oldest
ballet company,
showcasing classic
works..

THEATER RHINOCEROS

ℹ️ 2926 16th Street,
between Mission Street and
Van Ness Avenue

📞 415-861-5079

🚇 BART 16th Street; bus
14, 22, 33, 49, 53

The city's only gay
theatre. Check local
press for performance
details.

1000 VAN NESS

ℹ️ 1000 Van Ness
Avenue at O'Farrell Street

📞 415-922-4262

🚇 Bus 38, 42, 47, 49

14 screens of block-
buster Hollywood
nonsense, sometimes
with one film
dominating a couple
of the cinemas.

UNITED ARTISTS CORONET/METRO

United Artists Coronet

ℹ️ 3575 Geary Boulevard
at Arguello Street

📞 415-752-4400

🚇 Bus 33, 38

United Artists Metro

ℹ️ Union Street at
Webster Street

📞 415-931-1685

🚇 Bus 41, 45

A couple of
gorgeously restored
movie theatres that
have escaped San
Francisco's spreading
multiplex disease
are the United Artists
Coronet and United
Artists Metro. Both
gorgeous to look
at, the Coronet
even shows all the
latest blockbusters,
if you must. Grab
a mammoth bucket
of popcorn and
a soda, and sit
back and enjoy
the whole fabulous
experience.

Theaterland

Film Festivals

Pretty much whenever you're in San Francisco, there's bound to be some kind of filmfest taking place. Here are the best:

FESTIVAL CINE LATINO

📞 415-553-8140

🕐 Runs Sept

JEWISH FILM FESTIVAL

📞 415-621-0556

www.sfiff.org

🕐 Runs late July to early Aug

MADCAT FILM FESTIVAL

📞 415-436-9523

🕐 Runs late Sept

An alternative and independent women's film festival that attracts a lot of dyke celluloid action.

SAN FRANCISCO INTERNATIONAL ASIAN-AMERICAN FILM FESTIVAL

📞 415-252-4800

www.naatanet.org/festival/

🕐 Runs Mar

SAN FRANCISCO INTERNATIONAL FILM FESTIVAL

📞 415-929-5000

www.sfiff.org

🕐 Runs mid-Apr to early May

The 40-year-old film fest is the longest-running in America and shows over 200 films from a variety of countries and in every language imaginable. For more information, and to get those tickets in advance before they sell out (and they do), check out the Festival's website.

SAN FRANCISCO INTERNATIONAL LESBIAN AND GAY FILM FESTIVAL

📞 415-703 8650

www.frameline.org

🕐 Runs June

Film-festival-wise, this has to be the cream of the crop. It's one of the biggest and oldest in the world, and kick-starts all the Pride activities. It attracts filmmakers and visitors from all over the world, and rightly so.

The Film Festival kicks off Pride

Movies in San Francisco

With its sheer beauty and unique views, it shouldn't come as any surprise to discover that San Francisco has stolen the show in many movies over the past century. After all, it can do beaches, countryside, edgy downtown scenes and is less than 24 hours from Hollywood, meaning that on average 12 films a year are shot in the city. While films like *Bullitt, Vertigo* and *Escape from Alcatraz* automatically spring to mind, there's also a handful with a gay slant:

BASIC INSTINCT
Sharon Stone is the vampy bisexual murder suspect in this now notorious Hitchcock-alikey thriller. Check out the Stone flashing, Michael Douglas clubbing in a V-neck and some fantastic views of San Francisco.

Films for all tastes

INTERVIEW WITH A VAMPIRE
The Golden Gate Bridge and Market Street star alongside Brad Pitt and Tom Cruise in Neil Jordan's stylish adaptation of Anne Rice's vampire epic.

MRS DOUBTFIRE
Robin Williams drags up as a Scottish nanny with a little help from Harvey Fierstein in order to get close to his estranged kids. San Fran hotspots include the Transamerica Pyramid and views from his apartment on Washington Street.

STAR TREK IV – THE VOYAGE HOME
Gay anoraks get a double whammy when the crew of the Starship Enterprise get sent back in time to contemporary San Francisco to... erm... save some whales.

THE TIMES OF HARVEY MILK
Academy Award-winning film about San Fran's first openly gay city supervisor, Harvey Milk (see page 10), it might be a documentary but it's paced like a thriller! Narrated by Harvey Fierstein of *Torch Song Trilogy* fame.

WHAT'S UP, DOC?
One for Babs fans. Ms Streisand plays opposite Ryan O'Neil in this hilarious 1972 screwball comedy, which sees crazy mix-ups and a Buster Keaton-esque chase scene through the city.

Time for a swim

Working Out

After one night out in The Castro, you'll realise that gym culture in San Francisco is not just an afterthought; it's a way of life. Buffed-up boys are a common sight, and if you feel the need to pump some iron while you're in the city, there are some great gay-friendly gyms where you can get a day pass or short-term membership. As you'd expect, there are numerous workout spots in and around the Castro area, too.

OUTLINES

EMBARCADERO YMCA

🛈 169 Steuart Street at Mission Street

🌐 415-957 9622

🚇 BART Embarcadero; Muni Metro F, J, K, L, M, N; bus 2, 6, 7, 9, 14, 21, 31, 32, 66, 71

🕐 5.30am–10pm Mon–Fri; 8am–8pm Sat; 9am–6pm Sun

💲 $13 per day
Another branch at 220 Golden Gate Avenue, between Leavenworth and Hyde Streets

🌐 415-885-0460

This huge complex boasts a pool, exercise studio, well-equipped state-of-the-art gym and loads of fitness classes. Basically everything you'd ever

want from a fitness centre, but with views! It does tend to attract a Financial District crowd though, so if you're after something more true-to-life, then head to the YMCA in the Civic Center, which attracts a much cooler and more real local crowd.

EROS

🛈 2051 Market Street, between Church and Dolores Streets

🌐 415-864-3767
www.erossf.com

🚇 Muni Metro F, K, L, M; bus 35, 37

🕐 4pm–midnight Mon–Thu and Sun; 4pm–4am Fri–Sat

💲 $10 membership; regular entry $13; entry before 7pm $10; day pass (no membership) $17

There seem to be only a handful of saunas if

Let off steam

Workout around the clock

you're heading out of San Francisco, so thank goodness for this one on Market Street, which attracts a diverse Castro crowd, who all come to let off a bit of steam. You can even get a massage by appointment.

GOLD'S GYM

📍 2301 Market Street at Noe Street

📞 415-626-4488

🚇 Muni Metro F, K, L, M; bus 37

🕐 5am–midnight Mon–Thu; 5am–11pm Fri; 7am–9pm Sat; 7am–8pm Sun

💲 $10 per day; $38 per week

Possibly the most popular of all of The Castro's gyms, Gold's is part of a worldwide chain. That doesn't stop it from being welcoming and friendly, though. Packed to the rafters with some of the city's most well-formed bodies, it's a cheekily cruisey place for a gay crowd. Classes include aerobics, yoga, pilates, step and kickboxing, as well as some fine tuning for further abs definition and the like.

MUSCLE SYSTEM

📍 2275 Market Street, between Sanchez and Noe Streets

📞 415-863 4700

🚇 Muni Metro F, K, L, M; bus 37

🕐 5.30am–10pm Mon–Fri; 8am–8pm Sat–Sun

💲 $8 per day; $27 per week

Expect a slightly older crowd at this men-only, cruisey gym.

THE OSENTO BATHHOUSE

📍 955 Valencia, between 20th and 21st Streets

📞 415-282-6333

www.osento.com

🚇 BART 24th Street;

Muni Metro J; bus 14, 26

1pm–1am daily

$10–15

A bit of secret haven for the girls, this one. This Mission bathhouse is open daily and offers a relaxing range of treatments including saunas, hottubs, cold plunges and massage. An inexpensive and social hangout, it's a great way to meet the local girls.

STEAMWORKS

2107 4th Street, Berkeley

510-845-8992

BART Berkeley

A sauna in Berkeley if you decide to get out of town.

THE WOMEN'S TRAINING CENTER

2164 Market Street at Sanchez Street

415-864-6835

Muni Metro F, K, L, M; bus 37

5.30am–10pm Mon–Fri; 8am–8pm Sat–Sun

$8 per day; $27 per week

This is a friendly, helpful women-only gym which attracts a mixed/gay crowd of

serious workout enthusiasts.

WORLD GYM

260 De Haro Street at 16th Street

415-703-9650

Bus 19, 22

$10 per day

One of the city's best gyms, World Gym is mixed, but it does attract more men than women. With more than a whopping 35,000 square feet of space holding everything from Stairmasters up, this is where the serious fitness freaks come to pump iron.

All pull together

Sail away

Out of Town

As worth exploring as San Francisco itself are the areas and the islands around the city. Described below are places and things you can visit in a day on public transport and without too much hassle. If you really want to head out into some of the most beautiful Californian countryside and the famous wine areas of Sonoma and Napa counties, it's best to hire yourself a car, though Blue and Gold Ferries from Pier 41, Embarcadero (415-705 5555) do offer day trips.

Angel Island

ℹ Blue and Gold Fleet from Pier 41, Embarcadero **📞** 415-705 5555 **🚌** Bus 32, 42; cable car Powell-Mason **🕐** Two to three departures daily **🎫** Ferry: $10.50

Angel Island has worn a variety of guises over the years; Miwok Indians used to hunt there; it has been used as a quarantine and immigration station, and most recently a missile base. While tattered and derelict army buildings, most notably Camp Reynolds, still remain, the main reason to come here is for the wildlife and the captivating countryside. From the top of Mount Livermore, check out the 360-degree view of the Bay, San Francisco, Sausalito and Tiburon. All in all, a visit here is a

Exploring Angel Island

relaxing and peaceful way to spend half a day or so. Arriving by ferry at Ayola Cove, you can pick up a tram which will give you an audio-enhanced tour of the island, though the nicest way to check the island out is on foot or by bike. You can hire one at the cove. Recommended.

Berkeley

BART at Berkeley. By car: Drive over the Bay Bridge and turn north on Interstate 80 then follow signs.

Berkeley is famous for its university, and with good reason: the sprawling campus holds 30,000 students, 52 libraries and boasts 11 Nobel Prize winners. It is also justly renowned for being a site of political activity, when the 1960s saw it most famously at the forefront of the Civil Rights and Free Speech Movements.

You can easily spend a day in Berkeley, and it only takes about 30 minutes or so to get there on BART.

Once on campus, check out Sather Tower, otherwise known as the Campanile, for the view. Meanwhile, the University Art Museum, Palaeontology Museum, Bancroft Library and Botanical Gardens will appeal to anyone with specialist interests.

Running perpendicular to the campus is Telegraph Avenue, the area's main drag featuring student-friendly stores, cheap clothing outlets and assorted restaurants, as well as GAP and Tower Records. Look into Moe's Bookstore (tel 510-849 2087), which, not surprisingly in a student town, is a famous literary-fest.

Take the ferry out of town

Just as famous as its university is the town's 'Gourmet Ghetto', offering world-class food. A shout-out goes to internationally renowned and ever-popular Chez Panisse (tel 510-548 5525), which offers dinner downstairs and a café upstairs. Brave the queues.

That's not to say there's nothing to do if you're gay, though of course your choices are much more limited than across the bay in the city. Gay drinkerie Bench and Bar (tel 510-444 2266) and the sauna Steamworks (tel 510-845 8992) will start you off.

California Palace of the Legion of Honour

- Lincoln Park, Legion of Honor Drive at 34th Avenue and Clement Street
- 415-863 3330
- Bus 1, 1AX, 2, 18
- 9.30am–5pm Tues–Sun
- $8 adults, but free every Tues

Right across the city on the west coast is the California Palace of the Legion of Honour, arguably the prettiest museum in San Francisco thanks to its setting overlooking the Pacific Ocean, Golden Gate Bridge and the city itself.

Founded in 1894 by Alma De Bretteville Spreckels, the palace is home to an enviable collection of 87,000 pictures and sculptures which span 4000 years and highlight the ancient and European. Its big crowd-pleaser, however, is Rodin's sculpture *The Thinker*, which sits in the museum's Court of Honour. Its permanent collection is on the entrance level, but the gallery also houses temporary exhibitions.

Oakland

- BART at Oakland City Cente. By car: Drive over the Bay Bridge and follow sings for Downtown Oakland.

With some spare time on your hands, you might find yourself thinking about visiting Oakland. Don't. OK, so it might be relatively close and on the up, due to soaring property prices in neighbouring San Francisco, but there really is nothing of noteworthy importance to check out here. Jack London Square, named after the writer, is its prime tourist hot spot, but even its highlight is probably Tony Roma's Ribs.

Yes, there is a local gay scene here, but as Oakland's reputation is more than dodgy – in fact it's downright dangerous – you'd be well-advised not to be wandering the streets at night with a map and a guidebook.

Ocean Beach

Bus 5, 31, 38

Ocean Beach is the longest beach in San Francisco, located at and running along the western side of the city. It is very scenic and beautiful, but hardly the spot to take in some rays, as the weather tends to be cold and windy here. Likewise, the water is hardly appealing, and with its strong riptides you'll find that the only people brave enough to face it are local surfers. It is, however, the perfect place for a hearty walk.

Sausalito

Blue & Gold Fleet from Pier 41, Embarcadero   415-705 5555

Bus 32, 42; cable car Powell-Mason By car: drive over the Golden Gate Bridge on the US-101 and follow the signs.   Departures every 90 minutes or so

Ferry: $6 one-way.

Located just north of the Golden Gate Bridge and named by the

Seaside Sausalito

18th century Spanish explorers because of the 'little willow' trees found here, Sausalito is regarded as California's Mediterranean-like seaside village. You can make your own mind up about just how continental it is, but it is nevertheless very pretty and therefore crammed with tourists during the summer months.

Looking back at San Francisco

While it has a historic waterfront, thanks to a population of artists and writers, the emphasis here is on unique art galleries and shops – and even more glorious views of San Francisco.

Once again, don't be distracted by tourist food fare, and head inland to Caledonia Street to search out where the locals eat.

Tiburon

🚇 Blue & Gold Fleet from Pier 41, Embarcadero

📞 415 705-5555

🚌 Bus 32, 42; cable car Powell-Mason. By car: Drive over the Golden Gate Bridge and follow the US-101 north past Sausalito then turn right on Tiburon Boulevard.

🕙 Departures every 75 minutes, less frequent at weekends.

💲 $6 one-way

Leave from Pier 41

If you're going to pay a visit to one of the cutesy villages situated around San Francisco, your best bet is Sausalito. Tiburon, however, is worth a visit, as it is a picturesque and peaceful cosy little town with a couple of nice streets (Main Street and Ark Row) of restored 19th-century buildings as well as a handful of restaurants and the usual knick-knacky craft shops most tourists apparently can't get enough of.

The welcome at the W

Checking In

Like most tourist cities, San Francisco offers everything you could possibly imagine, and a lot more besides, when it comes to accommodation.

If money's no object, then lucky you! But if you're on a budget, choose very carefully. Most hotels cluster around Union Square and Nob Hill, though the cheaper ones are generally situated around the Civic Center, which is frankly shady, attracting homeless and hustlers alike.

Bear in mind that summer (May–Oct) is high season and that not only is it best to book in advance, but also that it's the most expensive time to holiday. All prices guides shown here are for double rooms, unless otherwise stated.

The Best Beds

Commodore

ℹ 825 Sutter Street at Jones Street. *Sutter Street/Jones Street: see map p. 40*
✆ 415-923-6800 fax 415-923-6804 www.thecommodorehotel.com
email commodorehotel@jdvhospitality.com
🚌 Bus 2, 3, 4, 76 |**🍴** **②** – **③**

Apparently, the neo-Deco stylings of the Commodore Hotel are meant to give the impression of a 1920s luxury liner. See what you think. Whatever, each of the spacious rooms, named after one of the city's 'hidden treasures', is colourfully fitted out and has walk-in closets, cable TV, tea and coffee facilities and anything else you might need. With both the Titanic Café, a classy little breakfast joint (*see p. 101*), and the Red Room (*see p. 107*) off its stylish lobby, you've got everything you need right on your doorstep. With fantastic staff too, this place comes highly recommended.

The following price guides have been used for accommodation, per room per night :

① = cheap = under $75

② = moderate = $75 – $200

③ = expensive = $200 and over

CHECKING IN

W Hotel

ℹ️ 181 3rd Street at Mission Street. *3rd Street and Mission Street: see map p. 46* 🌀 415-777-5300 fax 415-817-7823 www.whotels.com

Ⓜ️ Muni Metro: F, J, K, L, M, N; bus 9X, 14, 15, 30, 45, 81X 💼 ③

Groovy corner at W

One of several very, very swish hotels scattered across North America, and it doesn't disappoint. Walk in off the street and into a very *wallpaper* magazine-style bar – the bar upstairs changes colour and attracts a funky urban clientele. The perks: a delicious be-seen-at restaurant XYZ (see page 95), 423 deluxe guest rooms; oversized desks in each room with high-speed DSL internet access, cotton pique bathrobes, pillow top mattresses, feather beds, 250-thread-count and Egyptian cotton sheets, we're talking luxury here!

Styled on a 1920s luxury liner

Inn on Castro

ℹ️ 321 Castro Street, at Market Street. *Castro Street and Market Street: see map p. 70* 🌀 415-861 0321 www.innoncastro2.com Ⓜ️ Muni Metro F; bus 35, 37 💼 ②

The nicest and one of the most famous of all of the Castro's B&Bs, the Inn on Castro is just as colourful on the outside as on the inside. The rooms are a good size if at times a bit over-fussy or a tad wacky, but it's clean and the staff are really helpful and make you feel at home. On the quieter side of the Castro, it nevertheless has all the plusses of that location. With fresh plants and flowers, a smattering of modern art and a yummy breakfast, it'll make your gay stay all the more pleasant.

YHA

312 Mason Street, between Geary and O'Farrell Streets. *Mason Street and Geary Street: see map p. 20*

415-788 5604 fax 415-788-3023 www.norcalhostels.org
email sfdowntown@norcalhostels.org

Bus: 27, 38; cable car Powell-Mason; Powell-Hyde

If you must do San Francisco on a shoestring, you could do much worse than check into a youth hostel. OK, this YHA is overshadowed by a car park across the street, but it is literally a block from Union Square, and so is situated away from the degeneracy of Civic Center. There are straightforward rooms for two, three, four or five people, each with their own lock and key, so you don't have to worry about security. With all the other amenities hostels boast (kitchen, lockers, pay phones, nightly movies, group activities, etc.) and the bonus of no lock-out, you've got a pretty good find. No wonder it's very popular, so book up well in advance.

The Triton

342 Grant Avenue, between Bush and Sutter Street. *Grant Avenue and Sutter Street: see map p. 20*

415-394 0500
www.hotel-tritonsf.com

Bus 2, 3, 4, 30, 35

California suites

San Francisco is the home of the boutique hotel – a fancy turn of phrase for smaller-size independent hostelries that have a funky feel. The Triton, just outside the gates of Chinatown, is verging on the kitsch, but we like it. With a quirky little lobby and concierge with attitude, the gimmick here is the suites designed by Californian celebrities, including Carlos Santana and Jerry Garcia. Splash out for a suite and expect signature furniture pieces, air-and-water filtration systems and pure cotton linen. And don't forget the free Californian beer and wine served every evening in the lobby around 5pm. The Triton is meant to attract model and actor types, but don't hold your breath. Cool and funky in a great location.

Central YMCA

ℹ 220 Golden Gate Avenue, between Leavenworth and Hyde. *Golden Gate Avenue and Leavenworth: see map p. 56*
☏ 415-885 0460 fax 415-885 5439
www.ymcasf.org email hotel@ymcasf.org
Ⓜ BART Civic Center; Muni Metro F, J, K, L, M, N; bus 5, 16AX, 19
🛏

Admittedly, with Civic Center a stone's throw away, the Y is in a bit of a skanky area, but what it lacks in glamour it more than makes up for in decent budget hospitality, so no wonder it's popular with European travellers on a shoestring. There are shared dorms, while single and double rooms come simply decorated with a desk, sink and TV, but with shared shower facilities. You might want to bear in mind that no visitors are permitted, but with a free breakfast and complimentary use of the Y's extensive gym facilities thrown in, don't think you have to stay in a hotel to have a good time. Excellent value.

Palomar

ℹ 12 4th Street. 4th Street: *see map p. 20*
☏ 415-348-1111
fax 415-348 0302
www.hotelpalomar.com
Ⓜ BART Powell; Muni Metro F; bus 9, 16AX, 30, 45
🛏

Money always sniffs out money, so it's little surprise that here's the Palomar in San Francisco's up-and-coming ritziest area (the dot.com revolution happened just down the road) to give the W a run for its money. Billed as 'high-end style and service' with 'an urbane, sophisticated interior design', it's a to-die-for hotel experience, with all the loveliness happening upstairs and not totally evident from the lobby. The intimate bar and rated restaurant are already packing in non-resident San Franciscans, though they're missing out on their complimentary shoeshine and morning paper. Very nice indeed.

Chancellor Hotel

ℹ 433 Powell Street on Union Square. *Union Square: map p. 20* **☏** 415-362 2004 fax 415-362-1403 www.chancellorhotel.com **Ⓜ** BART Powell; bus 30, 38, 45, 76; cable car Powell-Mason, Powell-Hyde; **🛏 ② – ③**

Cracking value and an equally enviable location make this hotel an ideal home for anyone visiting the city for the first time. Situated off Union Square on Powell Street, with its upmarket stores and handy cable-car link to whisk you all the way to Fisherman's Wharf, the Chancellor's rooms are typical mid-range fare, more chintz than ritz but expertly serviced. Grab a room to the front if you can, and climb out onto the fire escape to take in the hustle and bustle of the big city. The hotel has its own bar and restaurant if you're too spent shopping to leave the comfort of its four walls. They often have great deals, so it's one worth checking.

Mandarin Oriental Hotel

22 Sansome Street. *See map p. 34.*

415-276-9888 fax 415-433-0289 www.mandarin-oriental.com/sanfrancisco
email reserve-mosfo@mohg.com

Bus 1, 12, 15, 30; cable car California

With prices to match its sky-high views, this hotel is no treat for
the faint of pocket – or those suffering from vertigo. If you have
the cash, then treat yourself to some of the most stunning views
you will ever see here. The hotel lobby and bar are situated on
the ground floor of the First Interstate Building downtown, with
the top 11 floors of the twin spires set aside for the Mandarin's
158 rooms. From the moment you check in and the maid brings
you a warm homemade cookie, the service is second to none.
Treat yourself to a Salty Dog in the bar and ride the elevator to
one of the glass walkways linking the two buildings for a
breathtaking view of the city spread out below. San Francisco
never looked so good!

The gay-friendly King George

Argent Hotel

The boutique Bohème

 50 Third Street at Mission Street
 415-974 8715 fax 415-543 8268
www.argenthotel.com
 BART Powell; Muni Metro F, J, K, L, M, N; bus 14, 15, 30, 35, 81X
 call for prices

Close to SFMoMA, this hotel has some stunning views of the Bay from its rooms with floor-to-ceiling windows. Lush surroundings, helpful staff, a great bar and restaurant, plus a garden for when the weather hots up, if you want to stay somewhere which is chic and stylish, then the Argent will do no wrong. The calibre of hotel means that the rates aren't published, so give them a call for availability and prices.

Red Victorian Bed, Breakfast and Art

Black and white on red

 1665 Haight Street at Cole Street
 415-864-1978
fax 415-863-3293
www.redvic.com
email redvic@ linex.com
 Bus 6, 7, 33, 37, 43, 66, 71
 ②

If you're not looking so much for a hotel as a San Francisco experience, then the Red Victorian Bed, Breakfast and Art will sort you out. Smack dab in the centre of Haight Ashbury, each room is wackily decorated and named to give you the true feel for this hippie homeland, hence the Redwood Forest Room, the Summer Of Love Room, the Japanese Tea Garden Room... d'ya get the idea yet?

You also might want to check out the meditation room for the whole shebang. Weird, but still kinda wonderful.

Sleeping Around

UNION SQUARE

HOTEL BOHEME

444 Columbus Avenue
415-433 9111 fax 415-362 6292 www.hotel boheme.com email mail@hotelboheme.com
Bus 12, 15, 41

Hotel Bohème is a gorgeous little boutique hotel in the North Beach area – kind of antiquey but more cool than chintzy. With 15 Beat-inspired rooms.

HOTEL MONACO

501 Geary Street at Taylor Street
415-292 0100
fax 415-292 0111
www.monaco-sf.com
Bus: 2, 3, 4, 27, 38

Another great hotel from the Kimpton Group, which boasts the Triton amongst others in its enviable portfolio, the Monaco is just two blocks from Union Square. Its amenities include a gym, and a cute little eaterie. French/kitsch in its styling, it's a fun place to stay, and there are some cheeky little additions, including a goldfish for each visitor upon request!

JULIANA HOTEL

590 Bush Street
415-392-2540
fax 415-391-8447
www.julianahotel.com
Bus 2, 3, 4, 9X, 30, 45; cable car Powell-Hyde

A cute little property not far from Union Square. Its bright, floral rooms attract a mixed straight/gay clientele. Clean and well run.

KING GEORGE HOTEL

334 Mason Street
415-781-5050
fax 415-391-6976
www.kinggeorge.com
Bus 38, 76

A gay-friendly traditional-style boutique hotel, with complimentary access to an offsite health club, affordable breakfasts and afternoon teas, and 142 mainly non-smoking rooms.

FINANCIAL DISTRICT

GALLERIA PARK

191 Sutter Street
415-781-3060
www.galleriapark.com
email reservations@ galleriapark.com
BART Montgomery;

Muni Metro F; bus 2, 3, 4, 30, 45

Within skipping distance of the shopping frenzy of Union Square, it claims to be a boutique hotel, but its décor is less *Wallpaper* and more stuffy and chintzy. The lobby, with free Californian wine in the evenings and jazz some of the week, is lovely, and the staff superb.

HOTEL GRIFFON

ℹ 155 Steuart Street
☎ 415-495-2100
fax 415-495-3522
www.hotelgriffon.com
email reservations@
hotelgriffon.com
Ⓜ BART Embarcadero;
Muni Metro F, J, K, L, M, N;
bus 14, 41

In the Financial District south of Market, just a couple of blocks from the Bay Bridge, this classily refurbished hotel is an upscale boutique affair with delicious views of the Bay from some of its rooms (six to be exact), as well as from the Red Herring Restaurant and Bar. Traditional touches, with a slightly modern twist.

PARK HYATT AT EMBARCADERO CENTER

ℹ 333 Battery Street
☎ 415-392-1234
fax 415-421-2433
www.parkhyattsf.com
Ⓜ Bus 1, 12, 15, 41, 42;
cable car California

Close to the Bay and within walking distance of downtown shopping, this chain hotel offers good standard rooms and swanky suites.

RUSSIAN HILL, NOB HILL AND TENDERLOIN

HOTEL EDDY

ℹ 640 Eddy Street
☎ 415 474-9219
Ⓜ BART Powell; Muni Metro F, J, K, L, M, N; bus 27, 31; cable car Powell-Hyde; Powell-Mason

Of all the cheap hotels, this is probably one of the best. With basic amenities, it's not going to deliver glamour – but in a dodgy area, you will at least feel safe inside.

HOTEL RENOIR

ℹ 45 McAllister Street
☎ 415-626-5200
www.renoirhotel.com
email sales@
renoirhotel.com

Ⓜ Muni Metro F, J, K, L, M, N; bus 5, 9

A functional hotel in a Flat-Iron-like building with seven floors of dark wood furniture and floral prints. It is gay-managed and says it has great views of the annual Gay and Lesbian Parade, but the area is hardly salubrious, with a selection of ropey fast-food chains and homeless folk just outside the door.

NOB HILL LAMBOURNE

ℹ 725 Pine Street
☎ 415-433-2287
www.nobhilllambourne.com
email nhl@
jdvhospitality.com
Ⓜ Bus 1, 30, 31, 38, 45;
cable car California, Powell-Mason, Powell-Hyde

This hotel offers comfy bedding, spa facilities and even workout equipment in the suites. Not far from Union Square, a luxury experience from folk who care.

PRESCOTT HOTEL

ℹ 545 Post Street
☎ 415-563-0303
www.prescotthotel.com
Ⓜ Bus 2, 3, 4, 38, 76

A fabulous four-star property with one of the best suites in the city, boasting a baby grand piano, hot tub and private terrace. Dig deep, as this is one of the best small hotels in the city.

RITZ-CARLTON HOTEL

ℹ 600 Stockton
☏ 415-296-7465
fax 415-291-0147
www.ritz-carlton.com
Ⓜ Bus 30, 45; cable car California

This upmarket hotel chain is in an historic landmark building, and as well as a swimming pool, it also has some amazing views of the city. Sophistication and grandeur. Very monied and very straight.

SERRANO HOTEL

ℹ 405 Taylor Street
☏ 415-885-2500
fax 415-474-4879
www.serranohotel.com
email reservations@serranohotel.com
Ⓜ Bus 27, 38
🛏 **②**

Another recently restored hostelry, complete with the odd Moroccan flourish. As with many of San Fran's cute boutique hotels,

there's a unique quirkiness, which includes being able to order board games with room service.

YORK HOTEL

ℹ 940 Sutter Street
☏ 415-885-6800
fax 415-885-2115
Ⓜ Bus 2, 3, 4, 27, 76
🛏 **②** – **③**

Gay/straight-owned hotel with a slightly kitsch feel. It's a bit chintzy, but a clean and spacious hostelry where scenes from Hitchcock's *Vertigo* were filmed. There's a gym and sun-drenched lobby.

CIVIC CENTER AND HAYES VALLEY

ABIGAIL HOTEL

ℹ 246 McAllister Street
☏ 415-626-6500
fax 415-861-9728
Ⓜ Bus 5, 19
🛏 **②**

Cutesy gay-owned hotel furnished with antiques, this attracts a mixed gay/straight clientele. Near the hubbub of Union Square and a mile from The Castro, the hotel offers breakfast and cocktails as well as lunch and dinner.

ALBION HOUSE INN

ℹ 135 Gough Street
☏ 415-621-0896
fax 415-621-3811
www.subtleties.com
email albionhouseinn@cs.com
Ⓜ BART Van Ness; bus 6, 7, 16AX, 66, 71
🛏 **②** – **③**

In Hayes Valley, this central hotel is quite twee but offers comfortable, clean rooms, great breakfasts and friendly staff. Check out the Joplin Room with its cute little roof deck; it's where singer Janis Joplin regularly stayed.

ARCHBISHOP'S MANSION

ℹ 1000 Fulton Street
☏ 415-563-7872
fax 415-885-3193
Ⓜ Bus 4, 21, 22, 24
🛏 **②** – **③**

There are 15 rooms in this hotel, in an old mansion house. Antiques and elegant furnishings abound. Spectacular, the Mansion offers breakfast and a complimentary wine evening. Romantic, with a great view across downtown.

PHOENIX

ℹ 601 Eddy Street
☏ 415-775-1380
fax 415-885-3109

CHECKING IN

 Bus 31

🛏️ ②

A hip and popular hostelry, the Phoenix's accommodation is based on 50s-style bungalows and boasts a pool. Within walking distance of the buzzing Polk Street and SOMA bar scene, it apparently plays host to visiting celebrities, but with rooms clocking in on the more affordable side, you're looking at D-listers for sure.

PACIFIC HEIGHTS

HOTEL DEL SOL

🛈 3100 Webster Street

📞 415-921 5520

fax 415-931-4137

www.thehoteldelsol.com

email del@
jdvhospitality.com

🚌 Bus 41

🛏️ ②–③

This boutique-style motel is a new addition to the accommodation scene. Its 57 rooms and ten suites are bright and colourful, and the complex even has a swimming pool. A unique bonus is that Del Sol offers free parking for its residents – almost unheard of in car-unfriendly San

Francisco – but which is just as well, as it's not in a great area for transport links.

HAIGHT ASHBURY

THE BELLA VISTA INN

🛈 114 Divisadero Street at Duboce Street

📞 415-255-3617

fax 415-552-2959

🚇 Muni Metro N; bus 24

🛏️ ③

More like cute little apartments than a hotel, the Bella Vista offers private suites complete with their own kitchen area, living rooms with fireplaces and colour TVs to a mixed crowd craving comfort. Close to Buena Vista Park.

THE HERB'N INN

🛈 525 Ashbury Street, between Haight and Page Streets

📞 415-553 8542

fax 415-553 8541

🚌 Bus 6, 7, 37, 43, 66, 71

🛏️ ①–②

A cute little B&B in the home of a brother and sister, the Herb'n (said with a silent 'H' – geddit?) Inn is within skipping distance of the Haight's coffee shops, *burrito* bars and

boutiques. A sweet little number, each of the three rooms is named after a different herb. There is a two-night minimum stay.

THE CASTRO

BECK'S MOTOR LODGE

🛈 2222 Market Street

📞 415-621-8212

fax 415-241-0435

🚇 Muni Metro F, J, K, L, M; bus 22, 37

🛏️ ②

These are pretty high prices considering it's not in the heart of the city, but if someone asked you to imagine a quintessential American motel, this is what you'd come up with, so yes, it's got a certain charm and is frequented mostly by gay gentlemen.

BOCK'S B&B

🛈 1448 Willard Street

📞 415-664-6842

fax 415-664-1109

🚇 Muni Metro N; bus 6, 43

🛏️ ①–②

This lesbian-owned B&B is in a cute Edwardian house in the Parnassus Heights area and is but a stone's throw from Golden Gate Park and the Haight. Attracting a mixed gay/straight clientele – there are only three rooms, however – it's a good 20-minute schlep from The Castro and even further from downtown.

CASTRO SUITES

927 14th Street
415-437-1783
fax 415-437-1784
www.castrosuites.com
email jmrscr@
castrosuites.com
Muni Metro: N; bus 24, 37

Right at the heart of Castro, these suites offer a 'home from home' style of accommodation for those of you who want to cater for yourself. This up-market apartment-style hostelry is gay-owned and run, and has a kitchen, bath-room and living room area in each of the stylish suites.

THE DOLORES PARK INN

3641 17th Street
415-621-0482
fax 415-621-0482
Muni Metro J; bus 22, 33

This luxurious guesthouse with four rooms and a suite nestles right next to the gorgeous Dolores

Park. A Victoriana residence decorated with period antiques, guests are requested to stay for a mini-mum of two nights, but it's worth it. One of the best hotels in the area.

ELAINE'S HIDDEN HAVEN

4005 Folsom Street
415-647 2746
www.sfhiddenhaven.com
email elaine@
sfhiddenhaven.com
Bus 24, 67

One for the ladies, this lesbian-owned B&B is one suite in a separate area from the owner's home. Clean, nicely private and homey, Elaine's attracts mainly lesbian punters.

THE PARKER HOUSE GUEST HOUSE

520 Church Street at 18th Street
415-621-3222
fax 415-621-4139
www.parkerguesthouse.com
email info@
parkerguesthouse.com
Muni Metro J

A luxury guesthouse in the Castro 'hood is a rare commodity, hence Parker's popularity. With

generous gardens and a steam bath, it attracts a mixed gay/lesbian clientele to its lovingly restored rooms.

24 HENRY

24 Henry Street
415-864-5686
fax 415-864-0406
www.24henry.com
email henryst24@aol.com
Muni Metro F, J, K, L, M; bus 37

This gay-owned and non-smoking B&B offers five stylishly upmarket rooms and a suite, just a few minutes from The Castro. The mainly male clientele enjoy the owners' hospitality and 24's peaceful location in a luxury Victorian setting.

THE WILLOWS

710 14th Street, between Church and Market Streets
415-431-4770
fax 415-4315295
BART Church Street; Muni Metro F, J, K, L, M; bus 37

A nice little B&B whose 12 rooms attract a gay clientele. Fresh flowers, break-fast in bed and friendly staff all add to the very pleasant overall experience.

Take a spin around the city but don't take a gamble...

Check This Out

Facts and tips for a stress-free visit

Getting There

BY AIR

There are three airports which serve the San Francisco and Bay area: San Francisco International Airport, San Jose International Airport and Oakland International Airport. The following airlines fly to San Francisco International Airport: American Airlines, British Airways, Continental Airlines, Delta Airlines, Northwest Airlines, Southwest Airlines, Trans World Airlines, US Air, United Airlines, Virgin Atlantic.

SAN FRANCISCO INTERNATIONAL AIRPORT
Most international flights arrive at San Francisco International Airport, which is thankfully the nearest airport to the city. You have several options how to get into the city.

BUS
The cheapest, least convenient and definitely the least glamorous way into the city is by two Sam Trans buses. The KX and 292 run every 30 minutes between the airport's upper level and the Transbay Terminal at 1st and Mission Streets. The bonus of this method is that you get a detour view of

the city as you enter, which is different.

Bus 292 costs the bargain price of $1.10 and takes an hour, while the KX costs $3 and takes just 30 minutes, but you're restricted to just one piece of carry-on luggage. Be wary of this after your stay, when your excess bags are bulging with Levi's, Nike trainers and Abercrombie and Fitch goodies.

PASSENGER VAN/ SHUTTLE BUS
Definitely easier than bussing it, but still quite reasonable in price, the rates range from $10 to $20 per person. The majority of vans leave every 15 minutes, so you shouldn't have any problem getting into the city centre. Remember to ask about discounted rates for two or more passengers.

Follow signs from the baggage claim area to the pick-up points reading 'Passenger Vans'. For your return journey, book a van at least 24 hours in advance. Your concierge can do this for you.

Companies frequenting the airport include: Bayporter Express (tel 415-467 1800); Bay Shuttle (tel 415-564 3400); Lorrie's Airport Service (tel 415-334 9000); Quake City Airport Shuttle

CHECK THIS OUT

(tel 415-255 4899); SuperShuttle (tel 415-558 8500).

TAXI

Now you're talking. Definitely the most convenient option, which you'll definitely pay more for, is a cab. Expect to pay about $35 plus tip for the 14-mile trip, and make sure you haggle for a flat rate. You'll find the pick-up points marked with yellow columns outside the baggage claim area.

SAN JOSE INTERNATIONAL AIRPORT

Frequented by the Silicon Valley dot.com boys and girls, this airport lies 60 miles south of San Francisco.

To get to the city take the Santa Clara transit bus 10 to Santa Carla CalTrain; it runs every 20–30 minutes and costs $1.25. Then take the CalTrain to San Francisco, which usually takes about 80 minutes and costs $4.75.

Unless you've got dollars to burn or a hefty expense account, forget taking a cab from here.

OAKLAND INTERNATIONAL AIRPORT

To get to San Francisco from the tiny Oakland Airport, which is across the Bay from the city, catch the Air-BART shuttle from the terminal to the Coliseum/Oakland BART station. It costs $2, and you'll need exact change for the ticket

machines. Trains run every 15 minutes from the central island outside terminals 1 and 2. Then catch the BART to San Francisco ($2.75). You really don't want to be doing this by yourself late at night, however, as Oakland can at times be unpredictable dangerous.

BY COACH

If you've been travelling around the States, you might be thinking of heading to San Francisco via a coach. The longest schlep for sure, it's not actually that much cheaper than catching a flight and is much more uncomfortable all told.

However, if you must do it by road, grab a Greyhound – it's the only long-distance bus operator to take you all the way to San Francisco from most major US cities. (tel 1-800-2222; www.greyhound.com).

If you're travelling from LA or Seattle to San Francisco, the alternative is the Green Tortoise bus, decked out with padded seating, bunk beds and a hi-fi system. Attracting younger

Take a taxi...

...or travel by bus

PASSPORTS AND VISAS

Under the United States' visa waiver scheme, visitors from the UK, EU (apart from Ireland, Portugal, the Vatican City and Greece) and Japan do not need a visa for stays, business or pleasure, under 90 days. A valid passport and an open/return ticket will be fine.

Canadians and Mexicans do not need a special visa to enter the country, but if you are driving over the border, expect to have your car searched. Again, taking your passport is essential.

CUSTOMS AND IMMIGRATION

Standard immigration rules apply to all visitors, which means it'll sometimes take an hour to get through those checks. During your flight, fill in the customs and immigration forms to present to an official when you land. Make sure you fill them in properly, or you'll find yourself at the back of the queue.

You'll probably have to explain the nature of your visit, and expect a grilling if you don't have a return ticket and not much cash with you, for obvious reasons.

WHAT YOU'RE PERMITTED TO TAKE INTO THE US

US Customs allow foreigners to bring in $100 worth of gifts before paying duty ($400 for American

travelling types, it's a cooler and more friendly alternative to the legendary Greyhound. In the summer months there's also a route to New York and Boston, which takes a staggering 14 days. Green Tortoise in San Francisco: 494 Broadway;. tel 1-800-8647.

BY TRAIN

Quicker than the infuriatingly slow coach, and definitely more com-fortable, the train's a cool way to get to San Francisco, with the bonus of a gorgeous landscape to take in. And hey, if you don't want to be stuck in economy, you could always take your own private cabin. Amtrak operates on a daily basis from most US cities – on the way you'll get a good look at the Rockies, the Nevada Desert and the imposing Sierra Nevada.

Catch the Coastal Starlight from LA for the stunning ocean views, as well as some dolphin and whale spotting. Contact Amtrak on www.amtrak.com. For details of rail travel from Canada, go to www.viarail.ca.

citizens), one carton of 200 cigarettes or 100 cigars, and 1 litre of spirits. No plants, fruit, meat or fresh produce can be brought in. Immigrant Assistance Line,tel 415-543-6767 (9.30am–5pm Mon–Fri).

WHAT YOU'RE PERMITTED TO BRING BACK TO THE UK

People under 17 cannot have the tobacco or alcohol allowance.
● 200 cigarettes; or 100 cigarillos; or 50 cigars; or 250g of tobacco.
● 2 litres of still table wine.
● 1 litre of spirits or strong liqueurs over 22% volume; or 2 litres of fortified wine, sparkling wine or other liqueurs.
● 60cc/ml of perfume.
● 250cc/ml of eau de toilette.
● £145 worth of all other goods including gifts and souvenirs.

If you bring something back into the UK worth more than the limit of £145, you will have to pay charges on the full value, not just on the value above £145.

IMMIGRATION ATTITUDES TO HIV-POSITIVE PEOPLE

Laws passed in 1993 can bar entry to persons who have been diag-nosed as HIV-positive. Non-US citizens who are HIV-positive are ineligible for a visa, and if you do tick the box that states you have a communicable disease on the visa waiver form, immigration officials have the right to refuse you entry.

Although no countries require HIV tests for casual tourists, most countries have ambiguous restrictions prohibiting entry of persons with 'communicable diseases'. I have never heard of a single problem from a traveller

with HIV or AIDS regarding border-crossing difficulty. Still, the potential exists.

If confronted about HIV medications, you might want to be prepared to tell officials that you have another non-communicable complaint – ask your doctor/clinic for advice on what to say.

In the City

TOURIST OFFICES AND INFORMATION

The Visitor Information Center is your best bet.

SAN FRANCISCO CONVENTION AND VISITORS BUREAU

ℹ️ Suite 900, 201 3rd Street
📞 415-974-6900
🚇 BART Montgomery Street; Muni Metro J, K, L, M, N; bus 12, 15, 30, 45, 76
🕐 8.30am–5pm Mon–Fri

Pick up loads of free maps and tat on all that San Francisco has to offer sightseeing-wise. There's also tons of information on hotels and restaurants.

VISITOR INFORMATION CENTER

ℹ️ Lower level of Hallidie Plaza, corner Market and Powell Streets
📞 415-391 2000 www.sfvisitor.org
🚇 BART Powell Street; Muni Metro J, K, L, M, N;
bus 6, 7, 8, 9, 21, 26, 27, 31, 66, 71
🕐 9am–5pm Mon–Fri; 9am–3pm Sat–Sun

Maps (some of which you'll have to pay for), coupons,

discounts and a hotel reservation service mean the Info Center has everything a visitor needs. Their phone number is a pre-recorded 24-hour 'what's happening' message, so for human help you'll have to go along in person. There is also internet access, starting at $1 for 5 minutes.

ACCOMMODATION

San Francisco has something for everyone accommodation-wise. Even though the city caters superbly to visitors, with over 30,000 rooms available, if there are conferences in full swing or if it's high season (June–Sept), you could find the city sold out. Booking in advance is always, therefore, a good idea.

Just because San Francisco is seen as *the* gay city in the US, as usual be sensible and use discretion when booking a room for you and your other half. If you want to be as 'out there' as you like, stay in one of the city's many gay hostelries. Chances are, though, that hotel reception staff and concierges will be of the homosexual variety anyway!

PUBLIC TRANSPORT

If you are planning on making use of the Muni, you're best off buying a one-day, three-day or seven-day 'passport', which you can use on most forms of transport, including cable cars. The pass will also get you discounts into some of the city's main tourist attractions.

Where to stay?

CHECK THIS OUT

BUSES

The best way to get around is by bus, and they'll get you where you need to go quickly and efficiently.

Fares are $1, and you'll need the exact change. Put your coins or dollar bill into the slot and ask for a 'free transfer', which is valid for two changes within a 90-minute period.

MUNI METRO STREETCAR

Almost like a cross between a bus and cable car, the trams are really efficient here.

Six of the lines (E, J, K, L, M and N) run underground in the downtown area – make sure you know exactly where you're going before you descend the staircase to the platform, as you're not given the luxury of a destination list or overview map, and different trains serve different routes even though they depart from the same platform. In the outer neighbourhoods, they run above ground.

Catch the cute F line at least once, as the trams are lovingly restored vintage streetcars. This route is also quite handy, as it takes you from the shopping area along Market Street up to The Mission and The Castro.

CABLE CARS

Almost as synonymous with San Fran as the Golden Gate Bridge, the cable cars were revived almost two decades ago and are the most amusing way to get around town – the only drawback is that they're full of tourists.

Muni metro

BART
(BAY AREA RAPID TRANSIT)

BART is the city's cool train system, which operates on four lines around San Fran and on to Daly City and the East Bay.

Buy your ticket from one of the vending machines and keep a hold of it if you don't want problems at the other end. Once again, be sure to know where you're going, as there's no map on the platform.

BART is marked by blue and white signs on street level. Tickets cost between $1.10 for one stop, one-way, and up to $4.30 for further afield.

FERRIES

One of the most enjoyable forms of transport in San Francisco, ferries will take you to some top tourist destinations: Blue and Gold Ferries, departing from Pier 41, run trips to Alcatraz, Sausalito, Angel Island and wine country.

The line also runs a commuter service to Oakland, Alameda, Tiburon and Vallejo, which you can pick up from the Ferry Building on Embarcadero at the foot of Market Street.

CAR RENTAL AND DRIVING

Unless you're planning on getting out of the city and exploring the Bay, renting a car to get you around hilly San Francisco is less a luxury than a real killjoy. The city is a nightmare for driving – it isn't a Steve McQueen experience, that's for sure, as the speed limit is a mere 25mph.

Street parking is at a minimum with lots of restrictions, so beware, and public garages are pricey. Parking tickets are easy to achieve.

If you must get yourself some wheels, give way to and steer wide of cable cars, park on hills in first gear and turn your wheels towards the sidewalk. And make sure everyone in the car belts up. Have I put you off yet? If you still want to persist, you'll need a credit card and a driver's licence to hire a car.

CLIMATE

San Francisco doesn't share the sunny blue skies that the rest of California basks in all year round. Practically surrounded by water, even on what is seemingly a warm day you can experience chill winds and the infamous heavy fog that rolls in over the Golden Gate Bridge to smother the city.

The temperature doesn't move much off the 18°C (60°F) mark in the day throughout the year, but watch out at night, when it drops dramatically.

SEASONAL VARIATIONS

Jan	High: 12°C	Low: 5°C
Feb	High: 15°C	Low: 7°C
Mar	High: 15°C	Low: 7°C
Apr	High: 17°C	Low: 8°C
May	High: 19°C	Low: 9°C
Jun	High: 21°C	Low: 11°C
July	High: 22°C	Low: 12°C
Aug	High: 22°C	Low: 13°C
Sep	High: 23°C	Low: 13°C
Oct	High: 21°C	Low: 10°C
Nov	High: 16°C	Low: 8°C
Dec	High: 13°C	Low: 6°C

CHECK THIS OUT

WHEN TO GO

The city can get ridiculously busy
in the summer months, so if you're
not in the mood to queue for
everything, don't even think
about it.

The best times to visit are late
May and June, or in late Sept and
Oct, when there are several gay
events to keep you busy,
including the naughty Folsom
Street Fair and the Castro
Street Fair.

EMBASSIES/ CONSULATES

Contact your embassy if you get
into trouble, have an emergency
or lose your passport. Note that
most are now restricted in exactly
how they can help you.

AUSTRALIAN CONSULATE
1 Bush Street
415-362-6160

BRITISH CONSULATE-GENERAL
1 Sansome Street
415-617-1300

CANADIAN CONSULATE TRADE OFFICE
555 Montgomery
415-834-3180

POLICE/CRIME

For ambulance, fire brigade or
police, dial **911**.

Home to one of the world's
biggest lesbian and gay popul-
ations, with over a quarter of the
city identifying as gay, lesbian or
bisexual,, the San Franciscan police
will be cool with the concept and
even have specialised task forces –

especially in the gay 'ghettos' of
Mission and Castro.

But as with all major cities, use
your head. Walking down an unlit
street in full Gucci gear and
swinging the latest Nikon camera
might get you in trouble, as it
would anywhere in the world.
Not many areas require caution in
the daytime, but be careful of
certain streets in The Mission and
areas to the east of the Civic
Center, which is where the city's
large homeless population
congregate. For the most part
they're harmless, but always act
with caution. You'll probably not
want to walk around these areas at
night.

If you do get into trouble,
contact the nearest police station
and make sure you get a reference
number for insurance purposes
and travellers' cheques refunds.

DRINKING

California's drinking laws are very
strict – no one under 21 is allowed
to consume alcohol anywhere.
Even if you look over 30, take your
passport out with you, because
however flattering it is to be asked
if you're over 21, if you can't prove
it, you won't get into a bar or club.

DRUGS

Despite this being the city where
the Summer of Love first began,
drugs are most definitely illegal
here. Anyone can get their hands
on them, and in certain areas
they're available freely, but be
warned – if you're caught with
them, kiss goodbye to the rest of
your holiday and perhaps even
your chances of entering the
country again.

POPPERS

Poppers can be bought in most clubs and sex shops and are legal to buy.

SMOKING

Smoking is a big no-no in San Francisco.

California has some of the most stringent anti-smoking laws in the world. You are not allowed to smoke in any of the following public places: lobbies, banks, sports arenas, elevators, bars, restaurants, clubs, shops, public buildings and on public transport. In other words, anywhere in an enclosed space. Some bars and clubs have smoking 'rooms' outside where you can puff away and invariably get chatting to the locals.

INSURANCE

You'd be crazy to visit America without any travel insurance. Full stop. It's well known that medical bills are phenomenal and that you could also wind up being slapped with a lawsuit if you're the cause of an injury-incurring accident.

HIV/AIDS AS A PRE-EXISTING CONDITION FOR TRAVEL INSURANCE

HIV and HIV-related illnesses may be considered pre-existing if the condition is not 'stable' 60 days prior to the purchase of insurance. Coverage can be tricky, because any change in medication, treatment or illness progression can be used to deny coverage.

Some policies treat HIV as a pre-existing condition, regardless of whether your treatment is 'stable' as described above. You would not be covered for cancellation or medical assistance for any HIV-related illness. However, if you broke your leg, you could be covered.

PRE-EXISTING CONDITIONS WAIVER

Mutual of Omaha began selling a tour and cruise travel insurance policy in 1995 that waives all pre-existing conditions. Travellers qualify for the waiver by purchasing the insurance within 24 hours of the time the initial trip deposit is made, and purchasing coverage for the full cost of the trip. Many other travel insurers now offer similar coverage.

No travel agent, insurance brochure or newsletter is qualified to define the terms of coverage for you; only the insurer itself, through the certificate of insurance or a dedicated phone service unit, can verify what is and is not covered. By all means buy insurance, but know what is covered before you go. If representations are made to you over the phone which are not in your written policy, demand written proof.

WHAT AMOUNT OF COVER TO CHOOSE

It's best to take out comprehensive travel insurance when you travel to the States. Make sure you have decent health cover, as medical expenses in America are renowned for being very costly.

VACCINATIONS

Vaccinations are not required to travel to San Francisco.

CHECK THIS OUT

WHERE TO FIND MEDICATION

You will have to pay for any emergency treatment, so contact the number on your travel insurance documents before you receive any. Your insurance company will direct you to a hospital that can deal directly with them. The following are emergency rooms (casualty departments) open 24 hours.

DAVIES MEDICAL CENTER
Castro Street at Duboce Avenue
415-565-6060

ST FRANCIS MEMORIAL HOSPITAL
900 Hyde Street 415-353-6300

SAN FRANCISCO GENERAL HOSPITAL
1001 Potreo Avenue
415-206-8111

UCSF MEDICAL CENTER
505 Parnassus Avenue, between Third and Hillway Avenues
415-476-1037

Other useful contacts:

GAY AND LESBIAN MEDICAL ASSOCIATION
415-255 4547 9am–5.30pm Mon–Fri

A professional organisation with over 2,000 gay, bisexual and lesbian physicians and students. As well as offering professional services, they also offer medical referrals.

PHARMACIES

Walgreens is the only 24–hour drugstore in the city. It has two branches: 498 Castro at 18th Street, and 25 Point Lobos Avenue.

GAY GROUPS AND RESOURCES

The age of consent in California is 18 across the board. There are gay support groups to turn to:

THE COMMUNITY CENTER PROJECT OF SAN FRANCISCO
1748 Market Street 415-437-2257
www.sfgaycenter.org/
Everyone welcome. Produces events and activities of interest to all members of the community.

GAY AND LESBIAN CENTER
Main Library, 100 Larkin Street at Grove Street 415- 557-4400

The Gay and Lesbian Center is a research building devoted to lesbian and gay history and culture.

HARVEY MILK INSTITUTE
Suite 451, 584B Castro Street
415-522-7200 www.harveymilk.org
Offers education opportunities to students in the gay community.

MEDIA

For up-to-date gay news and listings, check out San Francisco's free gay publications, which you can pick up at most bars and cafés. There are also free publications, which will give you the lowdown on what's on, where to eat and what to do. The best of these are *SF Weekly* and *San Francisco Bay Guardian*.

COMMUNICATIONS

You shouldn't have any problems using public telephones in San Fran – as usual, avoid using hotel room phones, as they'll punish you with hefty bills. If you want to

Pick up the local press

call home, it's best to purchase a phonecard ($6–$35). You can get them from most stores. You can also use your Mastercard with AT&T by dialling 1-800-225-5288. If you are dialling outside your area code, dial 1 + area code + the number.

Directory assistance is 411, operator assistance is 0 and long-distance enquiries are 1 + area code + 555-1212. Toll-free numbers start with 1-800 or 1-888.

INTERNATIONAL AREA CODES

Dial 011 followed by the country code:
  UK: 44;
  New Zealand: 64;
  Australia: 61;
  Canada: 1 + area code
  + telephone number

To call the US from outside the country, dial 001 plus the following area codes: San Francisco and Marin County 415; Oakland/Berkeley 510; San Jose 408; Napa, Sonoma and Mendocino 707

CURRENCY AND BANKS

One dollar ($) equals 100 cents (¢). Coins: 1c, nickel (5¢), dime (10¢), quarter (25¢) and the new one-dollar coin ($1). Notes, or bills, are similar in size and colour, so do be careful. They come in the following denominations: $1, $5, $10, $20, $50 and $100 – the $100 is often not accepted in smaller establishments.

If you have travellers' cheques, make sure you have ID with you to change them. You can also

CHECK THIS OUT

change travellers' cheques in exchange directly for your purchases, but ask first.

All major credit cards are accepted at most establishments. In fact, you may find it difficult to make a hotel reservation without one.

OPENING TIMES

San Francisco is far from being a 24/7 town. Bars can open at 6am and serve alcohol until 2am, and though dance clubs may stay open till 4am, they might revert to soft drinks from 2am. That's not to say, there are no all-nighters, but you might have to seek them out, you can check in the free papers.

Post offices open 9am to 5.30pm Mondays to Fridays and for limited times on Saturday, likewise most banks are 9am to 6pm Monday to Friday and limited hours again on Saturday though the city has loads of 24–hour Automated Teller Machines (aka cashpoints) so ready money shouldn't be a problem.

As to shops, typically they open their doors from 9am until 6pm Monday to Saturday and 10am to 5pm Sunday, yet you'll find opening hours tend to vary somewhat and there are occasional late night openings too. Best ring ahead.

PUBLIC HOLIDAYS

Americans don't get much more than two weeks holiday a year, but at least they have the following to look forward to:

1 Jan	New Year's Day
3rd Mon in Jan	Civil rights activist Martin Luther King Day
12 Feb	Former president Abraham Lincoln's Birthday
3rd Mon in May	President's Day
Sun, Mar or Apr	Easter Day
Last Mon in May	Memorial Day
4 July	Independence Day
1st Mon in Sept	Labor Day
2nd Mon in Oct	Columbus Day
11 Nov	Veterans' Day
4th Thur in Nov	Thanksgiving Day
25 Dec	Christmas Day

GAY EVENTS

There are a series of great gay events in San Francisco:

SAN FRANCISCO INTERNATIONAL LESBIAN AND GAY FILM FESTIVAL
www.frameline.org

The world's oldest and largest queer film-fest takes place before Pride every June.

GAY, LESBIAN, BISEXUAL AND TRANSGENDER PRIDE
www.sfpride.org

The city's month-long celebrations culminate in one of the world's biggest and best Pride marches at the end of June. The day before Pride is the unofficial Dyke March – a lesbian frenzy in and around Dolores Park. Boys aren't allowed.

FOLSOM STREET FAIR
A massive event, now with a 300,000-strong crowd, it was

initially aimed at the city's leather and S/M population, but now attracts locals, including straight families and clubbers. It takes place at the end of Sept and offers penny stalls, open-air clubs, DJs, bands, live performances and general debauchery.

CASTRO STREET FAIR

It's rainbow flags and buffed-up boys a-go-go at this 'community' fair. Live bands, arts and crafts and street vendors. First Sunday in Oct.

TIME

Pacific Standard Time is eight hours behind GMT.

ELECTRICITY

In the US, the voltage is 110-120V 60-cycle AC. Apart from shavers with dual-voltage flat-pin plugs, you'll need an adaptor for European appliances.

TIPPING

Tipping is not obligatory but is definitely expected, and folk in the service industry will shoot you some of the meanest dirty looks if you don't. Restaurants and taxis, 15–20 per cent of the total bill; bellhops $1–$2 a bag; in bars $1–$2.

At the tea dance

INDEX

INDEX

MY TOP RESTAURANTS

Fill in details of your favourite restaurants below . . .
Tell us about them by logging on to **www.outaround.com**

Restaurant _____

Contact Details _____

Comments _____

_____

_____

_____

Restaurant _____

Contact Details _____

Comments _____

_____

_____

_____

Restaurant _____

Contact Details _____

Comments _____

_____

_____

_____

My Top Restaurants

MY TOP BARS

Fill in details of your favourite bars below . . .
Tell us about them by logging on to **www.outaround.com**

My Top Bars

Bar _____

Contact Details _____

Comments _____

_____

_____

_____

Bar _____

Contact Details _____

Comments _____

_____

_____

_____

Bar _____

Contact Details _____

Comments _____

_____

_____

_____

MY TOP CLUBS

Fill in details of your favourite clubs below . . .
Tell us about them by logging on to **www.outaround.com**

Club _____

Contact Details _____

Comments _____

_____

_____

_____

Club _____

Contact Details _____

Comments _____

_____

_____

_____

Club _____

Contact Details _____

Comments _____

_____

_____

_____

My Top Clubs

AMSTERDAM
LONDON
MIAMI
NEW YORK
PARIS
SAN FRANCISCO

Out AROUND

Your Gay Guide to the World!

Look for the Rainbow Spine!